partners or an export boom. In each case he examines the relevance and explanatory power of the model under discussion. In most cases, these models were not very helpful in understanding the international trade experiences of small nations because small nations are a heterogenous group without uniform trade characteristics, and because many factors other than size and its associated characteristics have an important bearing on all problems considered. While these findings are negative, they will help avoid some spurious arguments about world trade problems and cures. On the other hand, some of the models offer valuable help in explaining aspects of some small economies. For example, other things being equal, smallness does tend to make countries more susceptible to large changes in the terms of trade and real income when the world demand or supply conditions for the commodities in which they trade change.

Mr. Lloyd's study is supported by an impressive amount of international trade literature. It collates many theoretical arguments and statistical facts concerning the trade of the countries under discussion. The author has also in some instances extended and modified the theories of international trade so that the significance of size and other variables can be tested. The findings are supplemented with extensive tables, and, the totality of this analysis competently serves the study of international economics.

Peter J. Lloyd was formerly senior lecturer in economics at Victoria University of Wellington and presently is assistant professor of economics at Michigan State University. He has published *The Economic Development of the Tourist Industry* as Research Paper No. 6 for the New Zealand Institute of Economic Research (Wellington, 1964) and other journal articles.

International Trade Problems of Small Nations

PETER J. LLOYD

International Trade Problems of Small Nations

DUKE UNIVERSITY PRESS   DURHAM, NORTH CAROLINA   1968

© 1968, Duke University Press
Library of Congress Catalogue Card number 67-28850
Printed in the United States of America

Preface

The subject of the behavior of the international trade of small countries has received scant attention. Yet country size is an obvious variable that may be an important determinant of some international trade flows and behavior. This book asks the question: Is it possible to develop a theory, or rather a collection of theories, of small nation trading? To this end, several models and arguments are presented and their relevance to small nations is debated. Where possible, empirical studies or statistics are used to confirm or refute hypotheses.

Some of the various models and arguments have been considered previously by different writers. Probably the oldest aspect of country size debated in the literature is the Classical argument that small nations obtain greater gains per unit of international trade than do large nations. This aspect is reviewed separately in Chapter VI. In the last few years some attention has been paid in small nations to the prospects and dangers of their joining customs unions or free trade areas in order to escape from the smallness of their own domestic markets. Other aspects, such as the small nation in a matrix multiplier model, have barely been mentioned before. Previous allusions to the various aspects of small nation trading are scattered widely throughout the literature. However, my searching revealed that, though piecemeal, these references are much more numerous than I expected at the outset. I have attempted to collate all previous references to the characteristics and behavior of small nations which are of any importance. A subsidiary part of this study is therefore oriented toward the history of these economic thoughts.

Much of the basic work for this study is contained in my doctoral dissertation submitted to Duke University in 1962. It should go without saying that I am indebted to the faculty of Duke University, especially my supervisors, Professors Calvin Hoover and Joseph Spengler, for their encouragement and many helpful suggestions. Without the generous support of the Duke University Commonwealth-Studies Center that enabled me to come to this country from New Zealand, this work could not even have been begun. Finally, I must thank Michigan State University for giving me the opportunity to revise my thoughts and, hopefully, to produce a more mature work.

Peter J. Lloyd

Michigan State University
October, 1966

Table of Contents

- I Introduction and Definition of Country Size   3
- II Trade Characteristics of Small Nations   14
- III Small Nations—Are They Unstable or Dependent?   36
- IV Foreign Trade Multipliers and the Balance of Payments in Small Nations   53

    Appendix to Chapter IV   66
- V Devaluation by a Small Nation   71
- VI The Small Nation in a Graham Model of International Trade   86
- VII Economies of Scale, Country Size, and Customs Unions   96
- VIII Summary and Conclusions   123

    Appendix I

    Analysis of Trade Ratios, 1963–1964   128

    Appendix II

    Analysis of Commodity Concentration of Exports, 1963–1964   131

    Index   134

List of Tables

II-1   Selected Small Developed Countries, 1964   32

II-2   Trade Statistics of Small Developed Countries, 1964   33

III-1 Direct Imports in Consumption and Capital Formation, 1960   38

III-2 Rates of Growth of Small and Large European and North American Countries   44

III-3 Approximate Ratio of Largest Export Market to Gross Domestic Product, 1964   47

III-4 Instability of Annual Export Receipts in Small Countries, 1946–1958   50

Appendices

I   Analysis of Trade Ratios, 1963–1964   128

II   Analysis of Commodity Concentration of Exports, 1963–1964   131

List of Figures

1   Trade Ratios and Country Size, 1964   25

2   Commodity Concentration and Country Size, 1964   28

International Trade Problems of Small Nations

CHAPTER I

Introduction and Definition of Country Size

This study was prompted by the belief that there may be certain characteristics which are common to the international trade of most small nations. One might expect, therefore, that there would be similarities in the balance of payments problems of these nations and that such events as the devaluation of the exchange rate or membership in a customs union would have similar effects on each of these small nations. Yet small nations have not generally received separate attention from writers in the field of international trade. This becomes especially obvious when compared with the quantity of literature on developing countries and numerous aspects of their international trade. Nowhere is there any systematic treatment of the characteristics and problems of the international trade of small nations which is comparable to that for developing countries. I have sought in this book to ascertain whether any consistent and useful set of propositions can be developed concerning the international trade of small nations.

The only other substantial discussion of size of nations and some aspects of international trade is contained in the proceedings of a conference of the International Economic Association held in Lisbon in 1957.[1] This conference concentrated on the effect of size on economies of scale and hence on per capita productivity and the stability of national income. E. A. G. Robinson noted in his introduction to these papers: "It is paradoxical that in the hundred and eighty years since [Adam Smith's] book was first published the relation of the size of nations to their economic prosperity and to their level of income per head has received comparatively little academic discussion. Both in the writing of papers and in their subsequent discussion many of us had a feeling of incredulity when we failed to discover a volume of antecedent literature such as the subject seemed to have deserved."[2]

---

1. *Economic Consequences of the Size of Nations*, ed. E. A. G. Robinson (New York, 1960).
2. *Ibid.*, p. xiii; see also pp. 15, 203.

Since this conference there has been some further examination of the relationship between economic size and levels of per capita income.[3] This aspect of size is outside the purview of this study, but what evidence there is suggests that national size and economies of scale do not have a significant influence on output per head, although Hollis B. Chenery in his important study found that, holding other factors constant, size had some effect on output per head in certain industries.[4]

It is worthy of note that the factor of country size has received very scant attention in other fields of economics. Only two cases are known to this writer. Chenery found the size of countries (using population as a proxy for market size) to be a significant determinant of the patterns of industrial development,[5] and in a recent book William G. Demas offers some ideas on the special difficulties small, densely-populated developing countries face in trying to achieve satisfactory and steady rates of economic growth.[6]

One probable reason little attention has been paid to small nations as a group is the difficulty of selecting a criterion for measuring the size of nations and of choosing the level of the criterion to distinguish small from large nations. This difficulty must be resolved before any empirical or theoretical investigation can take place. In this chapter I consider several alternative criteria and in so doing also discuss some simple ideas concerning the trade of small nations.

The most obvious and the oldest criterion is that of area. There is an old argument that a nation small in area may be presumed to be less well endowed with resources than nations geographically larger. More important from the point of view of international trade specialization, some authors contend "it is in the nature of things" that these

---

3. Edward F. Denison, *The Sources of Economic Growth in the United States*, Committee for Economic Development (New York, 1962), chap. xvi; Bela Balassa, *The Theory of Economic Integration* (Homewood, Ill., 1961), chap. v; D. S. Pearson, "Income Distribution and the Size of Nations," *Economic Development and Culture Change*, XIII (July, 1965), 472–478.

4. Solomon Fabricant, "Study of the Size and Efficiency of the American Economy," *Economic Consequences*, p. 47, W. A. Jöhr and F. Kneschaurek, *ibid.*, pp. 54–56, and Pearson, "Income Distribution," all failed to find any significant relation between the size of economies (population) and their per capita incomes. The main reason is that productivity in the same industries in different countries depends on many factors other than the scale of output; moreover, the average incomes in each country depend on the composition of their outputs.

The reference to Chenery is to his celebrated article, "Patterns of Industrial Growth," *American Economic Review*, L (Sept., 1960), 624–654. See comments in chap. vii, below.

5. "Patterns of Industrial Growth."

6. *The Economics of Development in Small Countries* (Montreal, 1965). For comments on this topic, see chap. iii, sec. i, below.

resources are likely to be less varied.⁷ Several economists have used this belief to explain why the industrial structure of small nations is likely to be more concentrated than that of large nations. Small nations, it is claimed, specialize in the production and export of a limited range of goods for which their resources are well suited. This position may be suitably described as the "narrow resource base" argument.

The inadequacy of this simple generalization is quite apparent. D. H. MacGregor declared that area should be expressed in terms of "productive area" rather than "total area," excluding all areas such as deserts and mountains which are of little use in producing goods.⁸ This proposition is in itself an admission that, particularly within countries large in area, resources may be so unevenly distributed that large sections are virtually barren. Conversely, one may expect that some small areas and some small nations may possess an unusually great range of resources in sufficient quantity to be able to produce a variety of products. At the Lisbon conference, K. W. Rothschild objected to the small area proposition because "it assumed that natural resources were randomly distributed over the earth's surface, and this was obviously not true. Resources such as climate, transport, and coal were highly concentrated." ⁹ Moreover, this measure of size ignores human resources and capacity to utilize the natural resources, which may be of overwhelming importance. These objections become more significant when one recalls the diversity of factors that are subsumed under "natural resources." Not only do they include mineral resources and land of varying quality, but they also comprise transport resources and locational factors. To take the last-mentioned alone, the European countries of Switzerland, Sweden, Norway, Denmark, and Belgium-Luxembourg, which are among those to be considered in later chapters, owe a large measure of their high levels of per capita production and their trade pattern to their fortunate proximity to the major European markets.

---

7. This naïve argument occurs in numerous places: Alfred Marshall, *Industry and Trade* (London, 1919), p. 23; D. H. MacGregor, "Trade of Large and Small Countries," *Economic Journal*, XXXV (Dec., 1925), 642–645; Bertil Ohlin, *Interregional and International Trade* (Cambridge, Mass., 1933), p. 258. It reoccurs in the Lisbon conference papers in several places: *Economic Consequences*, pp. 12, 17, 135, 226, 355. It has also been used in more recent empirical studies (see chap. ii, p. 14, n. 1, below, for references).

The appeal to metaphysics in the text above is from G. A. Duncan, "The Small State and International Economic Equilibrium," *Economia Internazionale*, III (Nov., 1950), 938.

8. "Trade of Large and Small Countries," p. 642.
9. *Economic Consequences*, p. 353.

Alfred Marshall developed other propositions concerning the area (size) of a country and the pattern of its trade. He stated that "a small country has a larger frontier in proportion to her area than a large country of the same shape."[1] This latter proposition may be expressed formally because of the geometry of size. Marshall notes that "areas of similar figures necessarily stand to one another in the proportion of the squares of their several linear dimensions."[2] For example, a circle whose area is one-fourth the area of another circle has a circumference only one-half that of the larger circle. Hence a smaller country generally has a larger frontier in proportion to its area and for this reason is likely to have a larger volume of trade per capita. A second geometrical property of small areas which in Marshall's view enhances this likelihood is that "the average distance of her people from the nearest foreign markets is likely to be less."[3] These favorable distance relations enable the export industries of small nations to compete more effectively with the domestic industries in the countries receiving these goods than may the industries of larger countries. Conversely, the producers of large countries have a greater competitive advantage vis-à-vis potential foreign imports than do those of smaller nations simply because of the longer haulage distances within a larger country.[4] In Marshall's view, these factors tend to increase the per capita value of small nations' trade relative to that of large nations.

These arguments of a geometric nature ignore many factors. When one takes into account the importance of internal distribution of population, transport resources, and—most important—the distance between countries, propositions such as Marshall's lose what little probability they had in the beginning. Finally, even if Marshall's propositions were true, transport costs are for most commodities a relatively minor item, usually less than 10 per cent of landed costs,[5] upon which Marshall placed a disproportionate emphasis.

Another favorite Neoclassical concept must be considered—"productive capacity." When many commodities are produced in a group of countries, this capacity has usually been interpreted as the ability

---

1. *Industry and Trade*, p. 25.
2. *Ibid.*, p. 25, n. 1. Marshall's emphasis on geographical area as the measure of size and the benefits of cheap transportation in extending the size of the market are directly in the tradition of Adam Smith; see also *ibid.*, pp. 23–27, and Adam Smith, *An Enquiry into the Nature and Causes of the Wealth of Nations*, ed. Edwin Cannan (Modern Library ed.; New York, 1937), Book I, chap. iii.
3. *Industry and Trade*, p. 25.
4. Simon Kuznets, "Economic Growth of Small Nations," *Economic Consequences*, p. 21, adopts this argument.
5. Charles P. Kindleberger, *Foreign Trade and the National Economy* (New Haven, 1962), p. 14.

of each country to produce, under complete specialization, quantities of one good selected as the index of relative "productive capacity" or national size. In practice it is impossible to measure this concept directly. Nevertheless, productive capacity has one distinct advantage over most criteria in that it is not, for the most part, affected by international trade. If one is to introduce nation size as a variable into a pure comparative advantage model, one requires a measure of nation size before international trade takes place. (Size and comparative advantage are discussed at length in Chapter VI, where it is concluded that some measure of productive capacity is the only feasible way of even defining size of nations in such models.) Frank Graham used this notion of size to deduce some very useful and illuminating conclusions concerning small nation trade. The Graham model discussed in Chapter VI illustrates the difficulties of incorporating nation size as a variable into formal international trade models and the necessity for precisely specifying the definition of size. Yet it also demonstrates that if the appropriate criterion is chosen, the factor of national size helps in explaining some features of international trade.

Productive capacity is not the same as national income. The latter measure is affected by the actual pattern of production and by the terms of trade established in addition to the productive capacity, in a general sense, of the countries concerned. However, provided the terms of trade are not unusually favorable to some countries compared to others in roughly the same range of productive capacity, the product capacity measure will in principle give approximately the same measurement of nation size as that of national income. Ex post national income can therefore be used as an approximation of productive capacity.[6]

What of national income as a criterion of national size? Another frequently heard assertion is that small nations suffer from diseconomies of small-scale production; that is, the size of the nation in some way does not permit producers in these countries to exhaust economies of scale in industries that require a large scale for most efficient or least-cost production. This supposed disability of small nations has been persistently raised as one pillar of the general arguments that small nations tend to produce only a few industrial products and to have a high commodity concentration in their export trades. (Effects of economies of scale on the pattern of international

---

6. Graham himself seems at times to imply that the best measure of size in his model is really national income *(The Theory of International Values* [Princeton, 1948], pp. 54; 91, n. 2). However, in the formal presentation of the model it is necessary to use the criterion of productive capacity.

trade are discussed in Chapter II.) Roughly the same set of ideas has been adduced in the thesis that large countries may be more efficient in terms of average output per head than smaller countries.[7] This "diseconomies of small-scale production" argument, as we may call it, is also a central concern in the contemporary discussion of gains and losses in the formation of customs unions and free trade areas (see Chapter VII).

In relating country size to diseconomies of small-scale production, size must in some way reflect or measure the size of the national markets, for it is the value of total production or expenditure that determines in part the size of the market for actual and potential products. Production for export may extend the volume of production beyond the domestic market level, a factor which is partly recognized in the national income criterion since the value of exported goods and services is one component of national income. Other factors, such as ease of internal transport, heterogeneity of tastes, and the presence of a subsistence sector, may restrict the size of the national market for goods. It is not possible empirically to adjust for these factors in many countries.

Most of the authors who have been concerned with this aspect of size did in fact choose national income, or preferably gross national product, as the criterion. There are obvious difficulties in the use of this measure. First, the national income is an aggregation of innumerable interrelated commodity markets. Solomon Fabricant notes that "no single measure, however, can adequately characterize the various dimensions of size that may be related to efficiency. Size of markets for goods, size of markets for productive factors, area and the character of resources embraced by it, population and its relation to area and resources—all these are involved. . . ."[8] The same writer states, nevertheless, that the "aggregate income or product of the American economy is the best available single measure of its size."[9] Admittedly it is true that the size of a nation affects, to different extents, the scope for realizing economies of scale in the production of different goods. However, the value of national income does limit the total range of goods produced.

Another basic objection that has been made to the measurement of size in terms of national income is that national income is an *ex post* magnitude, the result and the most common summary measure of the

---

7. *Economic Consequences*, Parts II and III. Other references to this topic were given earlier in this chapter.
8. *Economic Consequences*, p. 40.
9. *Ibid.*

nation's economic performance. It is therefore the reflection rather than the cause, it is reasoned, of the prevailing pattern of industrial production and international trade. C. D. Edwards has cautioned that "in considering the relation between the organization of industry and the size of the economy, we must beware of circular reasoning if we measure the economy from such an income standard; for the gross national product is probably affected by industrial organization, and it is difficult to separate the sequences that run from size to organization from those that run from organization to size." [1] That the efficiency of production and the extent of the market or the national income interact and are jointly determined is incontestable. Yet this does not preclude use of national income as the criterion of national size. It still remains that a small ex post national expenditure restricts the actual and possible production of goods requiring a large scale of production.

Some of the authors who believe that small nations are subject to diseconomies of scale employ population size as the criterion of nation size. Other writers who have discussed certain aspects of size and international trade have also used this criterion.[2] For a given population, or more precisely a given labor force, the size of the national income is determined by the average productivity per head.[3] However, the absolute population per se is not the only, or even the principal, determinant of average productivity. Since market size rather than population is of direct interest in this context, the national income criterion seems preferable. Only when one considers nations of similar per capita income may population be used as an indicator of the aggregate size of the market.

It should be evident by now that there is a multiplicity of possible criteria, none of which is universally serviceable. Various authors are concerned with various facets of "size." The basic reason for the use by different authors of different criteria in different problems (and on some occasions in the same problem) lies in the complexity of the ideas concerning size and its economic consequences. Several writers have employed dual or multiple criteria. At the Lisbon conference, L. Tarshis defined a large country as a country with "a large popu-

---

1. "Size of Markets, Scale of Firms, and the Character of Competition," in *Economic Consequences*, p. 117.
2. For example, Kuznets, in *Economic Consequences*; Michael Michaely, *Concentration in International Trade* (Amsterdam, 1962), chap. ii; Chenery, "Patterns of Industrial Growth." Kuznets, in his later study of international trade patterns, "Level and Structure of Foreign Trade: Comparisons for Recent Years," *Economic Development and Culture Change*, XIII (Oct., 1964), 1–106, reverted to the use of gross national product to measure national size.
3. In an open economy the terms of trade may cause national income and national product to diverge in real terms.

lation, a large area, a large variety of resources, and at least a moderately high level of income *per capita.*"[4] Leduc and Weiller considered size as having three major dimensions, namely the geographical dimension (natural resources and usable area), the demographic dimension (population), and the economic dimension (the size of the domestic market),[5] which they considered in turn. Marcy defined a small country as "one which, while depending comparatively heavily upon foreign trade both for supplies and sales markets, makes only a modest contribution to the aggregate flow of international trade,"[6] i.e., it has a high ratio of trade to national income and a low value of trade. This definition also implies that the country has a relatively small national income. An almost identical definition had been used previously by William A. Salant in his discussion of the foreign trade multiplier.[7]

These various aspects of national size are so diverse that it explains little to lump them together under the one general title of size. This practice was followed at the Lisbon conference where it was probably the outcome of the conference program. The title of the proceedings of the conference, "Economic Consequences of the Size of Nations," belies its intention. During the discussion of the papers many of the participants were aware of the overambitious nature of the program and called for a more intensive examination of specific issues.[8] They recognized that size in its various connotations was only one of many factors determining the level of average productivity of nations, the rate of economic growth, and the stability of national income. Indeed, one observer was so disheartened by the complexity of these problems that he declared "the size of a country by itself was economically meaningless."[9] The rather inconclusive results of their analyses are in large part attributable to their attempt to explain several aspects of the economies under consideration by recourse to one variable, national size. One should be able to do better by restricting the con-

---

4. "The Size of the Economy and Its Relation to Stability and Steady Progress: I," *Economic Consequences,* p. 191.

5. G. Leduc and J. Weiller, "The Size of the Economy and Its Relation to Stability and Steady Progress: II," *Economic Consequences,* p. 200; see also pp. 336–337. Demas, *Economics of Development in Small Countries,* pp. 41–43, employs these three dimensions.

6. G. Marcy, "How Far Can Foreign Trade and Customs Agreements Confer upon Small Nations the Advantages of Large Nations?" *Economic Consequences,* p. 268.

7. William A. Salant, "Foreign Trade Policy in the Business Cycle," in *Readings in the Theory of International Trade,* ed. H. S. Ellis and Lloyd Metzler (Philadelphia and Toronto, 1946), p. 214. See chap. iv, below.

8. See, for example, *Economic Consequences,* pp. 386–394.

9. E. Gudin, in *ibid.,* p. 388.

Introduction 11

sideration of national size to one field at one time and choosing the definition of size appropriate to the field, ignoring other ramifications of size in some sense.[1] Here, attention is confined to a number of specific and related features of the international trade of small nations in an endeavor to assess their importance. Furthermore, it is essential that the measure of size be single-valued and quantifiable, which in turn implies that the relevant concept of size has only one dimension. If size is given more than one dimension, the measurement of size involves an index problem and possible conflicts of ordering according to the several criteria.

Of all the criteria discussed the most serviceable appears to be that of national income. In all subsequent chapters national income will be used as a summary index of national size. The national income measure is the appropriate one in the discussion of diseconomies of small-scale production in small countries and the derivative arguments concerning instability and trade dependence in small nations. In the Graham model the measure of size is that of productive capacity, but in most cases national income would provide a very similar ordering of countries.

In most of the arguments put forward by earlier writers small countries have been supposed to behave similarly under certain circumstances not directly because they are small but because, being small, they supposedly have certain trade characteristics in common which lead to the predicted results. For example, the supposed high ratio of international trade flows to national product in smaller countries has been held to make these countries more unstable and to lower the values of their foreign trade multipliers, other things being equal. A high degree of commodity and geographic concentration of exports is also supposed to accentuate the instability of these countries. These arguments and their indirect connection with the size of countries are reviewed and modified in subsequent chapters. As a necessary prelude, multiple regression analyses are used in Chapter II to test the importance of country size (gross domestic product) as a determinant of two of the features of international trade relevant to subsequent models, namely, the ratio of international trade to national product and the degree of commodity concentration of export trade.

The use of national income as the single criterion of size means that a small nation may be either a nation with a relatively small population and a high per capita income or a nation with a large

---

1. E. A. G. Robinson comes to virtually the same judgment in summarizing the proceedings of this conference (*ibid.*, pp. xv, 391).

population and an offsetting low average per capita income. Some authors have felt it necessary to separate small developed countries from small developing countries.[2] Because of conditioning received from reading some of the vast literature on the special troubles of developing countries, one might expect the characteristics of a small developed country to differ substantially from those of a small and developing country. This is true in some instances, but the statistics analyzed in Chapter II demonstrate that developing countries are by no means uniform with respect to such features as the degree of commodity and geographic concentration of their export trades or the ratio of trade to national product and that many, though certainly not all, small developed nations have the characteristics usually ascribed to developing countries. On reflection this is not surprising since both small developed countries and developing countries are all small in the sense that they have a relatively small aggregate market size. Insofar as a small market is a determining factor of international trade patterns one would expect both groups of countries to exhibit the same characteristics. If per capita income per se is also a determinant of international trade, one can test this factor separately to ascertain its importance. In the next chapter the size of countries and five other independent variables, including per capita incomes, are used in the multiple regression analysis to see whether country size is in fact an important determinant of certain features of the international trade of some sixty countries of various sizes.

To discuss the behavior of small nations as a group in the models of subsequent chapters we must choose the critical value of the index of national size which is to separate small from large countries. The best solution would be to find some empirical bench-mark figure that represents a significant change in the associated characteristics of nations smaller or larger than this critical figure. For example, in his study "Economic Growth of Small Nations," Kuznets selected the absolute size of total population as his criterion and a population of ten million people as the dividing line between small and large, in the belief that most nations with a population larger than this figure exhibited certain characteristics that differ significantly from those prevalent in countries with a population smaller than this figure.[3] Other members of the Lisbon conference suggested that this bench

---

2. Kuznets, in *Economic Consequences*; Michaely, *Concentration in International Trade*, chap. ii.
3. *Economic Consequences*, p. 14. Michaely, in *Concentration in International Trade*, adopted the Kuznets bench mark.

mark was too low.[4] Any choice is of course arbitrary, especially if there is more than one critical level for the chosen criterion. At Lisbon some conferees spoke of "fifty million" nations, believing that this number as well as the ten million figure marked a critical level such that nations having larger populations were distinctive from those with smaller populations.[5] In Section III of the next chapter, I discuss and decide which nations are to be considered small.

Concern with the characteristics and behavior of small nations inevitably invites comparison with those of large nations. On some occasions comparisons are made. These are most extensive in the construction of the theoretical models of international specialization, the foreign trade multipliers, and in particular the devaluation of the currency of a small nation. The primary object of these chapters, however, is not to find whether small nations differ from large nations; rather it is the more limited examination of whether one can consider small nations as a distinctive group that exhibit a number of features in common and if so how these features may affect their behavior in certain circumstances.

The period I have in mind is the decade of the fifties and the early years of the sixties. In Chapters II and III, I have used data relating to the selected countries during all or part of this period; in later chapters I have relied more on case studies and examples.

---

4. *Economic Consequences*, pp. 349, 377.
5. *Ibid.*, p. xviii.

CHAPTER II

Trade Characteristics of Small Nations

I

It has been frequently alleged that small nations generally have the following three characteristics when compared with larger nations:[1] *(a)* a high ratio of international trade to national product, *(b)* a high commodity concentration in their export trade, and *(c)* a high geographic concentration in their export trade. It is also sometimes alleged that they should have a relatively low commodity concentration in their import trade. The essential principle of international trade is that each country specializes in the production, but not generally in the consumption, of the goods in which it enjoys a comparative advantage. Small nations specialize in the production and export of a more limited range of products, it is contended, and hence may be expected to import a greater variety of goods which are not produced domestically. However, two empirical studies have clearly shown that there is much less variation by country in the degree of concentration in import trade than there is in export trade and that there is no significant difference in import concentration indices between large and small countries.[2] Moreover, commodity concentration of import trade does not have the important implications that concentration of export trade has.

Similarly, Hirschman has suggested a factor that may lead the import trade of small countries to be more concentrated geographically than that of large countries. If the export trade of a small country is highly concentrated geographically and most of its exports are sold

---

1. References are too numerous for all to be given, but some important studies that have subscribed to one or more of these generalizations are Albert O. Hirschman, *National Power and the Structure of Foreign Trade* (Berkeley, 1945); W. S. Woytinsky and E. S. Woytinsky, *World Commerce and Government* (New York, 1955), pp. 62–68; Kuznets, *Economic Consequences;* Michaely, *Concentration in International Trade;* Kuznets, "Level and Structure of Foreign Trade." Woytinsky and Woytinsky, Kuznets in "Economic Growth," and Michaely used population as the criterion of size but considered developed and developing countries separately.

2. Michaely, *Concentration in International Trade,* pp. 13, 17–18; Kuznets, "Level and Structure of Foreign Trade," pp. 50–51.

to some large trading partner, the large country may by various means force the small country to secure the bulk of its import requirements from the large country.[3] This could have significant applications, for example, in the theory of tariff bargaining. On the other hand, the Swedish economist Anders Ostlind proposed a novel reason based on the lower non-discriminatory tariffs in small (European) countries as to why small countries should have a geographically dispersed import trade.[4] But again the lower value and smaller dispersion of the empirical indices of geographic concentration of imports ensure that there is no pronounced difference between the geographic concentration of imports in small and large countries.[5] We shall therefore confine our attention to the three important aspects of the structure of nations' trade. Each of these supposed characteristics is relevant to one or more of the models in later chapters.

Two complementary a priori reasons for expecting features *(a)* and *(b)* to be present have been put forward. They are the "narrow resource base" and the "diseconomies of small-scale production" arguments as they were labeled in the previous chapter. According to the narrow resource base argument, small countries, by virtue of their limited endowments and production possibilities, will produce and export only a few principal goods. On the other hand, large countries with a greater diversity of resource endowments will tend to have a diversified production and export trade relative to small countries. Further, the structure of demand and the range of goods demanded is likely to be similar in small and large countries, other things, especially the level of per capita incomes, being equal. Small countries will therefore tend to have a "relatively great foreign trade." Marshall, in formulating his ancillary geometric propositions, was primarily concerned with explaining why small countries often have a relatively high value of commodity trade per head.[6] For countries with similar incomes per head, this assertion is identical to the more usual statement that small countries tend to have a high ratio of international trade to national income.

Whereas the narrow resource base theory emphasizes the resource content of production and international trade in resource-intensive industries, the diseconomies of small-scale production statement em-

---

3. *National Power,* chap. ii.
4. Anders Ostlind, "Some Trade Dilemmas of Small States," *Skandinaviska Banken Quarterly Review,* XXXIV (Jan., 1953), 93.
5. Michaely, *Concentration in International Trade,* Table 3; Kuznets, "Level and Structure of Foreign Trade," Tables 10, 11.
6. Marshall, *Industry and Trade,* chap. ii.

phasizes the role of scale in capital-intensive manufacturing industries. Most writers who employ this argument simply presume that because certain industries require a large scale of operation for efficient production, the goods produced by these industries will not be produced by small nations.[7] By this they appear to mean that the nations are too small to provide a domestic market for the most efficient or least-cost output of the most efficient long-run plant. Certain industries must operate at a minimum scale or not at all, presumably because of large indivisibilities of plant. Those countries whose markets are too small to support this "technological" minimum scale will import such products from larger countries. It is contended that nations below a critical size seldom have such industries as an aircraft industry, an integrated automobile industry, or a large-scale chemical industry. In the opinion of Kuznets and others at the 1957 Lisbon conference, this critical size seemed to be a population of 10-15 million for developed countries.[8]

In a world in which some countries are considerably larger than others the existence of significant economies of scale in certain industries implies a technological determinant of the composition and direction of the foreign trade of countries that is still almost completely ignored by comparative advantage theorists. In his recent survey of international trade theory John S. Chipman notes:

> It is probably correct to say that economies of scale tend to be ignored in theoretical models not so much on empirical grounds as for the simple reason that the theoretical difficulties are considerable, and it is not generally agreed how they can be incorporated into a model of general equilibrium or whether they are at all compatible with the assumptions of perfect competition. That this is a poor reason for excluding them from consideration is evident, especially if it is true that they constitute one of the principal sources of international trade.[9]

What discussion there has been has centered almost entirely on the mathematical questions of stability and multiplicity of equilibria.[1] James Meade explicitly introduced country size into a model in which there are two countries, one large and one small (defining country

---

7. See, for example, Ostlind, "Some Trade Dilemmas," pp. 92–93, and John Jewkes, in *Economic Consequences*, p. 366.
8. *Economic Consequences*, pp. xvii, 17, 366.
9. John S. Chipman, "A Survey of the Theory of International Trade: Part II, The Neo-Classical Theory," *Econometrica*, XXXIII (Oct., 1965), 737.
1. See *ibid.*, pp. 736–749, and Richard E. Caves, *Trade and Economic Structure* (Cambridge, Mass., 1960), pp. 160–168.

size in terms of the quantity of resources), and two industries.[2] He has an interesting but very restricted analysis of the composition of international trade for a situation in which continuously increasing returns prevail in one industry but not in the second industry. Meade's analysis appears to be based on an identical case examined earlier by Bertil Ohlin.[3] Ohlin believed these cases in which the "most efficient scale is large compared to the need of the product" to be "probably not very important." [4] In any case this two-country, two-good model provides no insight into the complexities of multi-country, multi-good trade. In the general case the one definite conclusion of the pure theory of international trade on the pattern of trade is that "the presence of economies of scale of large scale production leads to multiple equilibrium, and therefore introduces an intrinsic arbitrariness into the determination of the international pattern of specialization and trade." [5] This is scarcely helpful!

One can at least say that the existence of decreasing cost industries producing tradable goods will increase opportunities for international trade and the total value of world trade itself, and therefore the trade ratios of trading nations. However, decreasing costs per se do not mean that the large countries will specialize in and produce all the output of the decreasing cost industries.[6] Access to markets in foreign countries enables small countries to escape the limitations of the smallness of their own markets and to realize the economies of scale in the industries in which they specialize.

Some secondary considerations will lead to the concentration of most of the output of these industries in large countries. Ohlin noted that industries subject to increasing returns will tend to be located in large nations if international transport costs are high.[7] This occurs simply because the high costs of transfer involved in exporting part of the large-scale production prohibit small countries from selling part of

---

2. James Meade, *Trade and Welfare* (London, 1955), pp. 351–356. A large country he considered to be one which is well endowed with much land, labor, and capital, and a small country as one endowed with relatively little land, labor, and capital (p. 351). Apart from the impossibility of measuring size in these terms, this does not imply, as Meade presumed, that the country large in this sense will also be large in terms of national income. This will depend on factor productivities and, when trade is admitted, on the terms of trade. It would have been preferable to define size in terms of national income.

3. Ohlin, *Interregional Trade*, pp. 55–56.

4. *Ibid.*

5. Chipman, "A Survey of the Theory of International Trade: Part II," p. 749.

6. Meade conceded this point in his two-country case; see also Caves, *Trade and Economic Structure*, p. 168.

7. *Interregional Trade*, pp. 146–147, 259–260.

their potential production in the markets of other (large) countries at a cost that would compete with a more favorably located large-scale production in those countries. Another factor that could restrict production of these goods in small countries is the "springboard thesis," which claims that production of these goods for export will not be undertaken without the secure base of a large home market. The greater political and economic risks of foreign sales may effectively prevent small countries from using export markets as an escape from the limitations of small-scale domestic production. At the Lisbon conference, V. A. Marsan contended that the most stable and profitable Italian exports are made up largely of a few mass-produced goods that have a sufficient domestic outlet in relation to the level of production, e.g., utility cars, motor scooters, and office machinery. Similarly, Tibor Scitovsky stated that "in England—traditionally an important export producer—today's rule of thumb seems to be that it is not prudent to rely on exports for more than 20-25 per cent of a company's total market outlet." [8]

A cursory acquaintance with economic history is sufficient to show that the "special" risks entailed in selling abroad and the absence of a large home base need not be decisive deterrents to export sales. For example, the export orientation of industry in Switzerland, a very small country, was strikingly illustrated at the same conference by the fact that in 1955 four major branches of industry—watches, chemical dyes, pharmaceutical preparations and perfumes, and embroideries—exported 95 per cent of their total output. Indeed, exports constituted over 50 per cent of sales in almost all major lines of industrial production.[9] Yet, at that same time, both Marcy and Robert Triffin regarded the risks attached to foreign trade as being so great for small countries that "trade liberalization is no longer enough. . . ." [1] They favored regional organizations such as customs unions to overcome these risks. Of course, any protectionist trade policies in the larger foreign markets will directly reduce the scope for using foreign trade

---

8. "International Trade and Economic Integration as a Means of Overcoming the Disadvantages of a Small Nation," *Economic Consequences*, p. 284. I have not checked the accuracy of this assertion. It is surprising since it was the specialization of eighteenth- and nineteenth-century England that led English economists to list the "extension of the division of labour" as one source of gain from trade. Adam Smith remarked that "by means of it [foreign trade] the narrowness of the home market does not hinder the division of labour in any particular branch of art or manufacture from being carried to the highest perfection" (*Wealth of Nations*, p. 415).

9. Jöhr and Kneschaurek, in *Economic Consequences*, Table IV, p. 63.

1. Marcy, *Economic Consequences*, p. 271. See also Robert Triffin, "The Size of the Nation and Its Vulnerability to Economic Nationalism," in *ibid.*, pp. 248-252.

as an escape from small domestic markets and associated diseconomies of scale.

This discussion has simply predicted that small countries may produce some, but a more limited number, of products in decreasing cost industries than may larger countries. By contrast, the discussion of partial liberalization of trade occurring in a customs union and the effect it may have on these industries has at least inquired into the main aspects of international trade in these goods. It has indicated the importance of the degree of competition prevailing before and after a union and the amount of product differentiation. The principal work in this field is Tibor Scitovsky's study of European integration.[2] The pure theory of free international trade almost invariably abstracts from all of these complications.

When local decreasing cost industries are protected from import competition, minimum size is an economic rather than a technological concept. In order for domestic production of a product to cease completely, an economy must be small in the sense that the market for a good is so small that even a single producer acting as a perfectly discriminating monopolist cannot secure what is considered an adequate profit on the capital invested. For any product the outcome will depend on the size of the domestic market in relation to the least-cost scales of production, as well as on tariff and import policies concerning import competition. Some indication of the diversity of results possible in international trade when one relaxes the usual assumption of perfect competition and non-decreasing returns is given by the discussion in Chapter VII of these factors in a customs union.

Fortunately, there is a more definite reason that the presence of economies of scale, internal or external, will certainly limit the range of goods produced in small countries. This lies in the definition of a small country as one in which the total value of all goods produced is small relative to other nations. Thus, even if a country is large enough to support at least one plant of the minimum economic size in some industries or if supplementary export trade permits a small country to produce some such goods, the total number and quantity of goods requiring large-scale production that can be produced in the country are limited by its total productive capacity. This limitation is probably the more important, except for those few industries requiring a very large scale of production for technological reasons.

Concern over products requiring a large scale of production becomes

---

2. *Economic Theory and West European Integration* (London, 1958).

particularly relevant when one considers capital goods industries. For the same reasons that small countries cannot produce a wide range of final products, they must import a large part of their capital goods requirements, both fixed capital goods and raw and semi-finished materials. Statistics presented in the next chapter show that the direct import content of fixed capital expenditure in most small developed countries is 40-60 per cent. From the export side, world trade data show that finished durable capital goods make up 20 per cent or more of the export trade of only five countries in the Western world—the United States, West Germany, United Kingdom, Sweden, and Switzerland—and that most of world exports of finished consumer goods and of finished producer goods originated in the few large developed countries.[3]

In addition to the narrow resource base and diseconomies of small-scale arguments, a third reason why small nations trading in a multi-country world tend to produce and export a narrow range of products is exemplified by the Graham model of comparative advantage discussed in Chapter VI. Small nations tend to specialize in the production of only a small number of goods in which they enjoy a great comparative advantage. This specialization is partly the result of the limited productive capacities of these countries and partly of the probability that small nations will have a smaller range of potential products for which the opportunity cost ratios are more widely dispersed than those of large nations. Small nations possessing a small productive capacity in relation to world demand for these products are able to specialize in the production of those goods in which they enjoy a great comparative advantage. This feature of multi-country trade enhances the likelihood—based on the narrow resource base and diseconomies of small-scale production alone—that the commodity exports of small countries will tend to be highly concentrated. While this feature has received mention by only one writer,[4] it is probably the most compelling of the three reasons which lead us to expect export concentration and high trade ratios in small nations.

One difficulty in the above reasoning is that the first pillar of these two propositions regarding trade ratios and concentration of export trade, the narrow resource base argument, relates to nations that are small in area, whereas the second pillar, the diseconomies of small-scale argument, relates to nations that are small in national income (or population, if the nations considered are similar in per capita

---

3. Kuznets, "Level and Structure of Foreign Trade," Appendix Table 7 and p. 62.
4. Kuznets, in *Economic Consequences*, p. 17.

income). Only to the extent that smallness in area is in fact associated with relatively small national income can there be any uniformly applicable set of propositions based on these two supports. Kuznets followed this procedure explicitly in the belief that "most nations that are small in population are also small in area." [5] The statistics in Appendix I reveal that the correlations between area and population or national product are not strong.[6] The narrow resource base argument was criticized in Chapter I, and less importance is attached to that argument than to the diseconomies of small-scale production and the above-mentioned feature of the multi-country Graham model. We are justified in applying these propositions to nations small in terms of national income.

The third feature of international trade attributed to small nations is the geographic concentration of their export trade. The dependence on the markets of one foreign country for a large part of total export receipts may mean that changes in the level of economic activity, the commercial policies, or trade agreements of that country have a profound effect on the dependent trading partner. Albert Hirschman pioneered this area in 1945 with his calculation of coefficients of geographic concentration of trade for forty-four countries.

According to Hirschman there are two a priori reasons for expecting a country with export trade concentrated in a few commodities to have a geographically *dispersed* export trade and vice versa.[7] A country specializing in the production of one good or only a few goods would be able to supply the whole world with this commodity or these commodities. Thus, commodity specialization should lead to geographic dispersion. Second, any country which traded largely with another single country would possess a comparative advantage in a large number of products and therefore the commodity concentration of its exports should be rather diversified. In this latter case, it is the geographic concentration that should induce a diversification of commodity exports. Moreover, the risks of geographic concentration may induce a country with a geographically concentrated trade deliberately to seek a more diversified commodity export trade among these countries to reduce such risks; presumably the converse also applies.

These propositions are unsound. A Graham model of multi-country trade shows that the only countries likely to specialize in producing

---

5. *Ibid.*, p. 16.
6. The actual simple correlation coefficient for the sixty countries between area and population is 0.49 and that between area and national product is 0.33.
7. *National Power*, pp. 30–31.

and exporting one or a few export goods are almost certainly small. There is no presumption that they will be able to supply the entire world with these products since their productive capacities are small. The precise pattern of world trade will depend on their productive capacities in relation to the size of world demand for these products. More than one country may produce and export these products. The small country may have an export trade that is highly concentrated both geographically and on a few products, and, conversely, any country with a large number of potential products and a large productive capacity may export a diversity of products to a number of countries. Hirschman's apparently logical propositions illustrate the danger of thinking in the framework of two-country models, a practice which Graham vehemently attacked.

It is not so surprising then that Hirschman and later Michaely found that countries whose export trades are concentrated geographically also tend to have a high commodity concentration in their export trade.[8] They suggested two factors which tend to produce this association of high commodity and high geographic concentration of exports: low level of industrialization and long distance from the major world markets.[9]

II

In the previous section several arguments were presented to explain why small nations may be expected to have three trade characteristics. Does the empirical evidence support the three hypotheses? To test the first two related hypotheses concerning trade ratios and export concentration, two sets of multiple regressions were performed for some sixty countries, using as dependent variables the ratio of international trade to national product (Y_1) and the degree of commodity concentration (Y_2). In each case six plausible independent variables were used. For the trade ratio regression the independent variables were gross domestic product (X_1), gross domestic product per capita (X_2), the degree of industrialization (X_3), population (X_4), area (X_5), and fixed capital formation as a percentage of gross domestic product (X_6). Population, area, and gross domestic product were suggested by arguments above concerning size of country (measured in different

---

8. *Ibid.*, p. 106, and Michaely, *Concentration in International Trade*, pp. 20–25.
9. Hirschman, *National Power*, p. 107, and Michaely, *Concentration in International Trade*, p. 23.

ways) and international trade.[1] Fixed capital formation was included because of the possible effect on the ratios of the high import content of expenditure on capital formation in most countries. Per capita incomes were included chiefly because it is commonly believed that the ratio of trade to national product is usually higher in developing countries than in developed countries.

The degree of industrialization was included because it has been claimed elsewhere that industrialization should lower the trade ratio.[2] This traditional argument is based on a dubious vertical pattern of exchange of manufactures for primary products and raw materials. A counterargument, essentially the same as that concerning the size of nations, would suggest that the more diversified the industrial structure the greater the opportunities for international trade and, other things being equal, the greater the trade ratios.[3] The measure of industrialization I employed was the statistics from the United Nations *Yearbook of National Accounts Statistics* of the percentage of gross domestic product produced in the "Total Industry" sector, that is, the ISIC commodity groups 1-3 (Mining, Quarrying, and Manufacturing) and 5 (Electricity, Gas, and Water). This seemed the most suitable measure of the extent of general industrial development outside the agricultural sector. Although the United Nations warns that these statistics are "not fully comparable from country to country in coverage and classification used," [4] the discrepancies do not appear to be large. Were more reliable information available on the structure of industrial production in a large number of countries and on the consequent possibilities of engaging in international trade, the importance of this factor could be more thoroughly explored.

The ratio of exports of goods and services to domestic product shows the share of output produced in the export sector, and the ratio of imports of goods and services to domestic product shows the proportion of income expended on imports, if one ignores the import content of exported goods and services and excludes all transit and re-

---

1. While variable 2 is the ratio of $1 \div 4$, there is little multicollinearity between these variables, and all three variables may be used.

2. These views are discussed by Karl Deutsch and Alexander Eckstein, "National Industrialization and the Declining Share of the International Trade Sector, 1890–1959," *World Politics*, XII (Jan., 1961), 267–299, and Robert E. Lipsey, *Price and Quantity Trends in the Foreign Trade of the United States* (Princeton, 1963), chap. ii.

3. The complex effects of industrial growth on international trade patterns for a small sample of countries are amply discussed by Alfred Maizels, *Industrial Growth and World Trade* (Cambridge, Eng., 1963), chap. iii.

4. United Nations, *Yearbook of National Accounts Statistics*, 1965, p. 465.

export trade. The ratio of the sum of exports plus imports of goods and services to domestic product is the best summary measure of the extent of a country's involvement in international trade. Statistics of both international trade flows and domestic product are taken from the United Nations *Yearbook of National Accounts Statistics* so that the trade and national product statistics are as far as possible consistent among countries. The numerator of the ratio for each country is total exports plus imports of goods and services; the denominators are the recent United Nations estimates of gross domestic product, all converted to U.S. dollars by the use of purchasing power parity exchange rates.[5] Robert E. Lipsey has shown that in the United States when the effect of changes in the prices of imported goods relative to those produced domestically is removed the historical trade ratios in real terms give "a very different picture" from the current value ratios.[6] The same distortion due to different relative prices of traded and non-traded goods could be serious in cross-country analysis. The United Nations estimates of purchasing power parity rates are the only ones available for many countries, and we must use them. Data for these ratios and the six independent variables refer to 1963 or 1964 with few exceptions. The data were available for sixty countries that together comprised over 90 per cent of world trade, excluding that of the Sino-Soviet bloc, and presented a wide sample of countries in all continents (see Appendix I).

A linear regression of trade ratios on the six independent variables was fitted because the stated propositions suggest that the trade ratios should increase directly with increases in the percentage of gross domestic product (GDP) expended on gross capital formation and decrease with increases in the size of country (GDP), GDP per capita, population, area, and degree of industrialization. Marshall's area propositions would make these ratios a quadratic function of area, but little significance can be attached to his propositions.

The regression equation and standard errors obtained were:

$$\hat{Y}_1 = 0.295147 - 0.000008\, X_1 + 0.000251\, X_2 + 0.000042\, X_3 + 0.000185\, X_4$$
$$(0.133180)\quad (0.000003)\quad (0.000095)\quad (0.003806)\quad (0.000193)$$
$$- 0.000035\, X_5 + 0.010431\, X_6;\ R^2 = 0.2666.$$
$$(0.000022)\quad (0.007085)$$

Of the six variables only two are significant at the 5 per cent level:

---

5. Hereafter, all dollar amounts are given in U.S. dollars.
6. *Price and Quantity Trends*, p. 43.

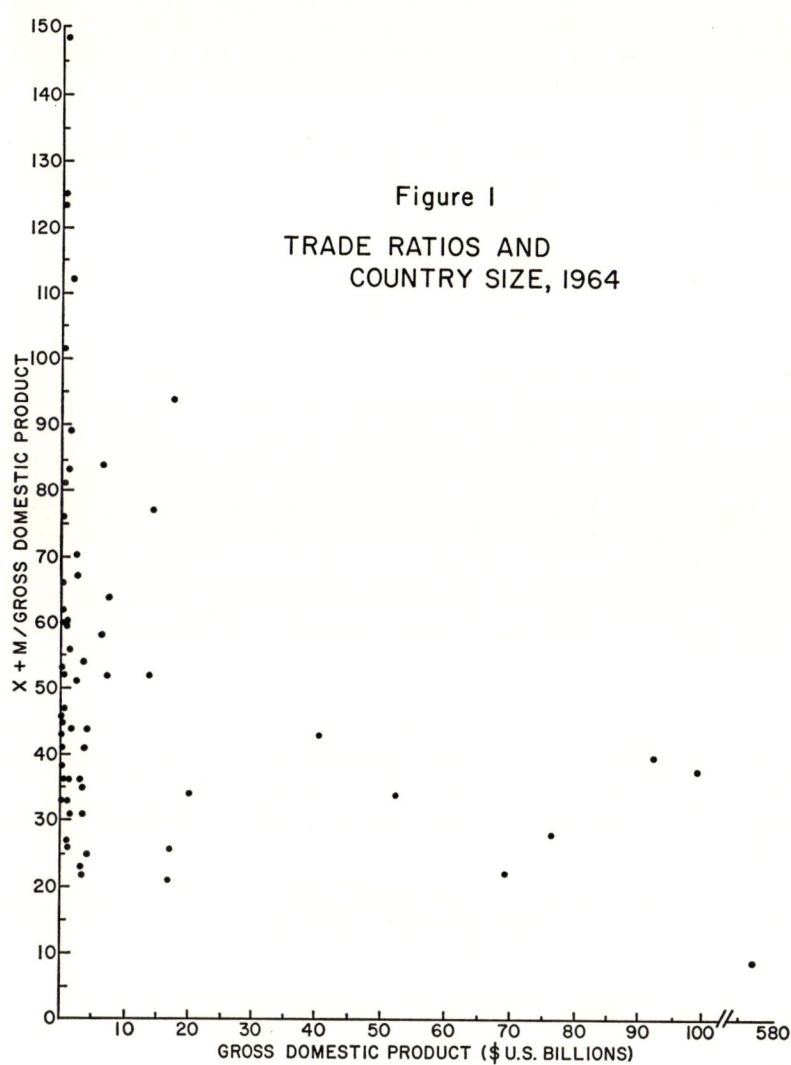

Figure I

TRADE RATIOS AND COUNTRY SIZE, 1964

the size of the country (X_1) and gross domestic product per capita (X_2). The negative association between the trade ratios and GDP is in the direction expected but the positive association with per capita incomes is the reverse of that suggested. It is no doubt based on the higher level of trade in manufactures among richer industrial countries.

The multiple correlation accounts for only 27 per cent of the variation in the trade ratios among the sixty countries,[7] but this is not really surprising. There are certainly errors in some of the data, especially those based on estimates of gross domestic product and their components. These data errors reduce the regression and correlation coefficients but these disturbances should not be great. Undoubtedly the fundamental explanation is that the factors explaining patterns of international trade are many and varied. Several possibly important factors were omitted—location of countries on trade routes, proximity to major markets, access to major markets, historic trade ties, differing degrees of government encouragement to export and import trade, and exchange rate overvaluations, to name only a few obvious influences. One should not expect any aspect of a phenomenon so complex as international trade among many countries to show any significant covariation with a single variable or even several variables.[8] The scatter diagram in Figure 1 shows the lack of association between GDP and trade ratios. Indeed, the trade ratios of small countries whose GDP's were less than $20 billion are fairly uniformly distributed over the 10-120 range.

For the linear regression of indices of commodity concentration of export trade (Y_2) on six independent variables, the total value of the export trade of the countries concerned (X_7) was substituted as a possible explanatory variable for capital formation as a percentage of gross domestic product, which is inappropriate in this test. Data for 1963–1964 (Appendix II) were available for sixty-two countries, fifty-one of which were included in the first regression. The measure of the degree of commodity concentration used is a truncated version of the Hirschman Index of commodity concentration;

$$100 \sqrt{\sum_{i=1}^{n=4} \left(\frac{X_{ij}}{X_j}\right)^2}.$$

X_j is the total value of country J's commodity exports and X_{ij} is its exports of commodity i. Commodities were defined as the three-digit SITC commodity groups.[9] This index is a weighted summary measure

---

7. All the simple correlation coefficients, including that for the size of the country, are very low; the highest is that for fixed capital formation (0.28) because of its auto-correlation with GDP per capita and to a lesser extent with GDP.

8. The failure of single and multiple variable analysis to explain much of another aspect of international trade—the degree of year-to-year instability in total export receipts—has been observed and carefully documented by Joseph D. Coppock, *International Economic Instability* (New York, 1962), chaps. v and vi.

9. For a discussion of the problems of defining a commodity in international trade, see Michaely, *Concentration in International Trade*, p. 7.

of the export shares of the four main commodities in each country, and it varies between limits of zero and one hundred. For our purposes, it is clearly superior to a concentration ratio for the largest one, two, three, or four commodities in that it is affected by the share of all four main commodities, each share appropriately weighted by itself.[1] It also avoids the problem with concentration ratios of choosing an arbitrary number of commodities when there is a low correlation among these different concentration ratios, as is certainly the case in international export trade. The index was truncated at the level of the four main commodities in each country to avoid the tedious calculation of shares for as many as 150 commodities in each country. The construction of the index insures that the truncated index is a good approximation of the true value. In no case was the share of the omitted fifth-most-important commodity as high as 10 per cent of total exports; that is to say, the inclusion of this commodity would have added considerably less than 1.00 to the index in every case. The understatement of the true values of the indices will tend to be proportionately greater for those countries with lower commodity concentration; the truncated indices will therefore overstate the differences in the degree of commodity concentration of exports among countries, but this exaggeration is slight.

The second regression equation is:

$$\hat{Y}_2 = 57.09820 + 0.00005\,X_1 - 0.02480\,X_2 + 0.03971\,X_3 - 0.01161\,X_4$$
$$(5.94891) \quad (0.00007) \quad (0.00724) \quad (0.26308) \quad (0.00429)$$
$$+ 0.00218\,X_5 - 0.00060\,X_7;\ R^2 = 0.4388.$$
$$(0.00133) \quad (0.00151)$$

The results of this regression resemble those of the first regression on trade ratios. In this second regression, GDP per capita (X_2) and population (X_4) are the only two significant variables. Gross domestic product by itself has a virtually imperceptible and insignificant effect on the degree of commodity concentration of a country's exports. The six variables together account for a slightly higher percentage (44 per cent) of the total variation in commodity concentration than in the trade ratio regression.[2]

---

1. The properties of the index are elaborated by its original discoverer: Hirschman, *National Power*, Appendix A. Statistically it is determined by the coefficient of variation and the number of observations. Hirschman used it to measure geographic concentration of trade flows, but it has since been used by Kuznets, Michaely, and Coppock to measure commodity concentration.

2. The highest simple correlation coefficient in the second regression is that with GDP per capita (0.586).

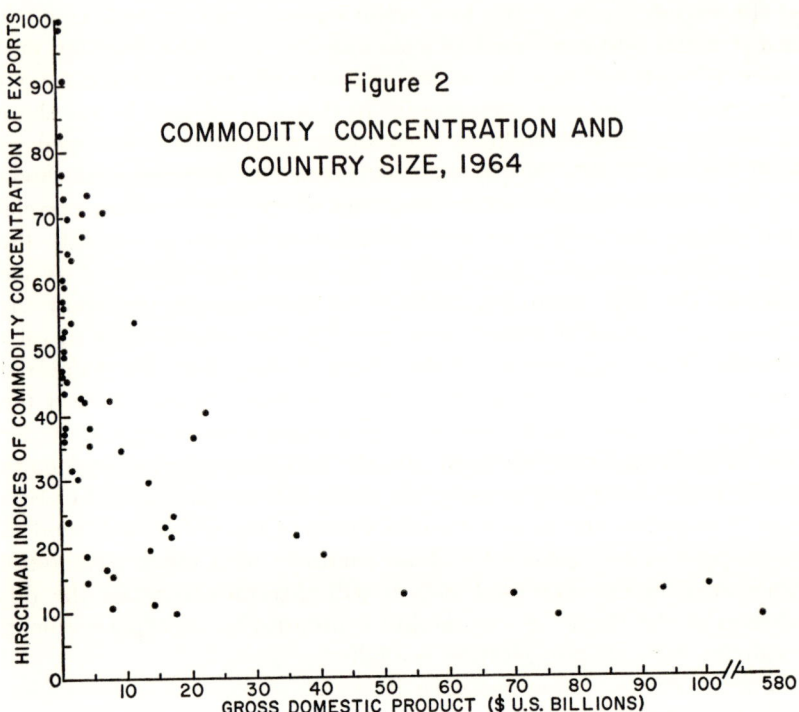

Figure 2

COMMODITY CONCENTRATION AND COUNTRY SIZE, 1964

From the scatter diagram in Figure 2 we see that indices of commodity concentration for all small countries whose gross domestic products were less than $10 billion in this scatter were evenly distributed between the limits of zero and one hundred. In this diagram, six of the seven countries whose gross domestic products were $10–$20 billion had a lower than average degree of commodity concentration.

These two multiple regressions have revealed that size of country as measured by gross domestic product (and the same conclusion applies for the population or area criteria of size) has little effect per se on a country's trade ratio or the degree of commodity concentration of its exports. In the past others have claimed to have found a relationship between size of country on the one hand and trade ratios and the degree of commodity concentration on the other, but they have done so only when grouping all countries into a few broad groups.[3] These groupings have hidden the wide variation about the group averages. These authors have also considered the effect of na-

---

3. Kuznets, in *Economic Consequences* and "Level and Structure of Foreign Trade," pp. 11, 53–54; Michaely, *Concentration in International Trade*, p. 16.

tional size separately among developed and developing countries, thereby removing a part of the effect of variations of per capita incomes which they considered to be important, but this procedure does nothing to remove the effect of all the other variables which may be equally important. A multiple regression which simultaneously tests several variables is definitely preferable to this technique.

These regression results need not mean that the size of a country is altogether unimportant. Examination of the scatter diagrams suggests another aspect of size. Both the trade ratios and the indices of commodity concentration of export trade of all countries whose gross domestic products are less than $10 billion are distributed widely about the average for all countries. However, the commodity concentration of all countries whose domestic products exceed $10 billion—with the sole exception of Brazil—is below the average (42.6). Similarly, all countries whose national products exceeded $20 billion have below average trade ratios (54). It seems, therefore, that a large country will have a relatively low trade ratio and a relatively low degree of concentration in its export trade, while a smaller country may have either a low or a high trade ratio and index of concentration of export trade depending on many circumstances concerning its location, access to major markets, resource endowments, etc. The critical size in 1963–1964 was apparently a domestic product of more than $10–$20 billion.

The results do mean that one cannot assert that small countries tend to have certain characteristics. In general they do not because the effect of size is swamped by many other factors. This suggests the possibility of selecting those countries having all the characteristics in which we are interested rather than examining all small countries or all developing countries or any other group of countries which are supposed to have these characteristics. One would then consider the models of devaluation or the foreign trade multiplier and other models as developed in later chapters as relating to precisely those countries which actually have these characteristics. Unfortunately, this promising approach is not possible because there are relatively few countries which have both a high degree of commodity concentration in their export trade and a high trade ratio (to consider only the two features of international trade discussed so far in this chapter). Consider the top third of the fifty-one countries common to both regressions obtained by ranking them in descending order by their trade ratios and by their indices of commodity concentration. Many of the seventeen countries which rank in the top third according to the commodity concentration of their export trade have among the lowest trade ratios of all countries considered in these regressions: Chile, Columbia, and Vietnam have trade ratios of less than 30 and Iran has a ratio of only 35. Conversely, many of the top seventeen countries when ranked by their trade ratios have particularly low indices of commodity concentration: Netherlands, Norway, and Belgium-Luxembourg have indices of commodity concentration of below 20, Ireland has an index of 31, and Cyprus an index of 37. This list of exceptions, even in this sample, is too numerous to allow us to assume that a high trade ratio is usually associated with a high degree of commodity concentration of exports. This finding alone destroys part of the foundation of the general theory of small nation trading.

The most exact course would be to test each of the models for only those countries in each case which have the relevant attributes. However, this would mean that the group of countries to which one might apply one model—for example, the devaluation model—would be different from the group discussed in relation to another model such as that of the foreign trade multiplier. Moreover, in two models (the Graham model of comparative advantage and the customs union model), the size of country variable is introduced directly rather than indirectly by means of its association with the trade ratio or one of the other trade characteristics. It seems worthwhile to examine the extent to which the various models and arguments are applicable to a group of small countries.

The procedure to be followed in the following chapters is first to restate the various arguments and models and then to confine empirical investigation to small developed countries. This group is used partly because some of the international trade models to be considered were proposed with small developed countries in mind, partly because this procedure avoids the possible confusion of the effects of smallness with the effects of low per capita incomes, and partly because of the author's interest in seeing whether this group of countries may behave similarly in like circumstances. Our concern now is with small nations alone rather than with the broader question of comparing small nations with large nations. Unless otherwise indicated all subsequent references to small or large countries may be understood as referring to small or large developed countries. But I shall at times indicate the close parallels in the development of some theories concerning the trade difficulties of small developed countries with ideas and theories relating to developing countries. These parallels are most noticeable in the recent debates on the formation of customs unions and in views of the causes of instability in export receipts.

III

The group of small developed countries was selected in the following way. First, I considered only those countries which in 1964 had a per capita income of $700 or more as estimated by the United Nations, which has converted the gross domestic product of each country into U.S. dollars by the use of purchasing power parity exchange rates. These, in some cases, differ considerably from the official pegged rates. (Among the countries finally selected this conversion entailed a 50 per cent depreciation from the pegged rate for Finland and a 30 per cent appreciation for South Africa.) These exchange rates and the statistics of national products themselves are subject to several well-known sources of possible error but the cutoff of $700 insures that all countries selected are well developed in terms of per capita incomes. Next, I established the upper limit for small countries, in terms of their gross domestic products, at $20 billion. This figure was suggested by the previous discussion of commodity concentration and trade ratios, and it also accords with a common-sense classification of developed countries as small or large.[4] Australia was actually a fraction above this limit at the end of the period but it has experienced a rapid growth of real gross domestic product in the postwar period and for most of this time was clearly a small country by this criterion. At the lower end of the GDP scale two countries—Iceland and Kuwait—were excluded. Iceland, with a 1964 GDP of $350,000, was much smaller than all the other countries included, and Kuwait, despite its high average per capita income, must be regarded as very underdeveloped in terms of industrial development or the per capita income of the bulk of the population. Soviet bloc countries were excluded because the foreign trade of these countries has been subject to strict state control which has severely limited the amount and dictated the direction of trade.

Table II-1 lists, in descending order of size, the fifteen countries selected and basic data pertaining to them. These countries are a homogeneous group in several respects. All had GDP's in 1964 of $2.5–$20.1 billion and populations of 2.5–17.5 million. Although the statistics are not presented, all have manufacturing or processing sectors which, while small by comparison with the major European and North American industrial countries, are more developed than those of the great majority of developing countries. For most of the postwar

---

4. Chenery, "Patterns of Industrial Growth," suggests that economies of scale appear to be significant in some industries in a market up to about ten million people at U.S. income levels, i.e., up to about $30 billion (p. 646).

period all except South Africa have had populations of less than the fifteen million which was suggested at the Lisbon conference as a critical level dividing small from large industrial powers. Indeed, all

Table II-1 SELECTED SMALL DEVELOPED COUNTRIES, 1964

Country	GDP at factor cost ($U.S. billions)	GDP per capita ($U.S.)	Population (millions)
Australia	$20.1	$1,807	11.1
Netherlands	17.4	1,431	12.1
Sweden	16.0	2,095	7.7
Belgium-Luxembourg	14.3	1,472	9.6
South Africa	13.7	700	17.5
Switzerland	12.2	2,071	5.9
Denmark	8.0	1,684	4.7
Austria	7.5	1,033	7.2
Norway	7.0	1,882	3.7
Venezuela	6.7	792	8.4
New Zealand*	5.2	2,046	2.6
Finland	4.2	923	4.6
Israel†	2.7	1,084	2.5
Ireland	2.6	895	2.8
Puerto Rico	2.5	963	2.9

*New Zealand statistics for gross domestic product and GDP per capita relate to 1963.
†Israel's gross domestic product has been converted into U.S. dollars at the official exchange rate.
Source: United Nations, *Yearbook of National Accounts Statistics*, 1965, Table 9B.

except South Africa and the Netherlands had populations of less than ten million for almost all this period. The similarity of per capita incomes and populations removes most of the separate influence of these two variables on their international trade patterns. In these respects they are a homogeneous group. Of course the countries differ markedly in other respects which may be relevant to the problems we examine later, e.g., rates of growth and rates of population increase, size of government sectors, overseas capital borrowing or lending, and rates of inflation. Three of these countries have had special handicaps in the postwar period. Finland lost 9 per cent of its pre-World War II territory, Austria was occupied for ten years, both of these countries paid substantial reparations, and Israel has been engaged in border disputes since its inception.

One should observe, however, that these countries are small only by comparison with the large developed countries whose national products exceed $20 billion. Their total productive capacities are certainly small alongside that of the United States whose GDP in 1964 was measured at $576.8 billion. On the other hand, Australia in 1964 ranked as the ninth largest country in the Western world in terms of gross domestic product in equivalent U.S. dollars, and the Netherlands, Sweden, and Belgium-Luxembourg all exceeded in aggregate size of production such countries as Indonesia, Brazil, Pakistan, and Nigeria which are all very much larger in terms of population. (The population criterion of size when applied to all countries, developed and developing, gives quite a false ordering of countries by market size.) Nevertheless, all fifteen countries certainly fit the usual ideas of smallness for developed countries.

Because of their greater homogeneity, these fifteen small developed countries might be expected to exhibit greater uniformity in their trade characteristics than all the countries small in terms of GDP which were included in the multiple regressions. The following table presents the statistics for the three trade characteristics with which we are concerned.

Table II-2 TRADE STATISTICS OF SMALL DEVELOPED COUNTRIES, 1964

Country	Trade ratios	Hirschman Index of export concentration	Share of largest partner in exports (percentages)	Largest partner
Australia	34	36.69	18.3	United Kingdom
Netherlands	94	9.60	26.9	West Germany
Sweden	52	17.82	14.3	West Germany
Belgium-Luxembourg	77	11.37	22.9	Netherlands
South Africa	52	19.14	31.5	United Kingdom
Switzerland	60	18.32	16.3	West Germany
Denmark	64	15.66	23.1	United Kingdom
Austria	52	10.81	27.1	West Germany
Norway	84	16.77	20.1	United Kingdom
Venezuela	58	70.72	33.9	United States
New Zealand	47	43.83	49.5	United Kingdom
Finland	44	38.07	22.4	United Kingdom
Israel	67	40.65	14.5	United States
Ireland	70	30.64	72.0	United Kingdom
Puerto Rico	112	N.A.	N.A.	United States
Mean of all countries in regression	54	42.6	N.A.	

Sources: Cols. (1) and (2): Appendices I and II. The Hirschman Indices for Sweden, Switzerland, and New Zealand which were not included in the regressions were calculated from the same source. Cols. (3) and (4): United Nations, *Yearbook of International Trade Statistics*, 1964, Country Tables; statistics refer to merchandise trade only.

It is clear that the trade ratios vary widely. Contrary to the alleged pattern, all the countries, with the exceptions of Venezuela and New Zealand, have below average indices of concentration in their export trade. One noticeable feature is that the Continental European countries, especially the Netherlands, Belgium-Luxembourg, and Norway, have trade ratios that are well above the average together with indices of commodity concentration that are among the lowest of all countries. Both their location in the largest trading market of the world and their membership in either the European Economic Community (EEC) or European Free Trade Area (EFTA) tend to raise their trade ratios and lower the degree of commodity concentration in their export trade, which suggests that the factors of location and market access may be more important determinants of the patterns of world trade than is generally recognized. It also suggests that the association of high ratios with small countries—in these cases at least—is partly spurious. Similarly, the high trade ratios of Ireland and Puerto Rico are explicable mainly by their preferential access to the markets of the United Kingdom and the United States respectively.

What of the geographic concentration of the export trade of these countries? Again the empirical realities are more complex than the hypothesis suggests. Table II-2 lists the share of the largest partner alone for the fifteen small developed countries. Since the chief concern here is with the political and economic risks of having a large number of one's eggs in the one basket, the simple share of the single largest export partner seems preferable to the more sophisticated Hirschman Index of geographic concentration in this context. Of the fifteen countries only two, Ireland and New Zealand, depended on one market for approximately one half or more of their total sales. In both these cases the primary explanation is obviously their historical connection with the British market, bolstered for most of their recent history by significant though declining margins of Imperial Preference and guaranteed access to the United Kingdom market for their major food exports. The dangers of excessive reliance on one market are well illustrated by the experience of New Zealand at the time of the United Kingdom's application in 1961 to join the European Economic Community. Before this application was vetoed by France, the New Zealand government had desperately sought and obtained assurance from the United Kingdom and the European Economic Community that her vital agricultural exports to the United Kingdom would be protected by a unique "special arrangement."

The other eleven countries have surprisingly low geographic concentration ratios. Of the non-European countries, the relative importance of the United Kingdom to Australia and South Africa is a historical association. Venezuelan trade with the United States exemplifies the importance of particular commodities, in this case, petroleum and iron ore. Similarly, Danish trade with the United Kingdom consists predominantly of dairy products. The low values of all Continental European countries, like the low commodity concentration of their export trades, are due to their fortuitous location. This factor has been accentuated since 1958 because of the more rapid expansion of intra-area trade within the EEC. Although the statistics are not cited here, many, but by no means all, of the developing countries depend on one large foreign market for 50 per cent or more of their export sales. The explanation for many of these countries, especially in Africa, lies in their ex-colonial or cultural ties with France and the United Kingdom.

The results of the multiple regressions for some sixty countries and the statistics for a group of fifteen small developed countries indicate that size of country may play a part but not a dominant part in the determination of trade ratios, commodity and geographic concentration of export trade. Many small countries do not in fact have the characteristics that have often been ascribed to them, because the significance which country size may have is swamped by the influence of location, market access, historical ties, the level of the exchange rates, and many other factors. This also means that the group of small developed countries to which most of our attention is confined in the subsequent chapters does not generally have all the trade characteristics which the builders of the models believed small countries to have. Essentially in these chapters we proceed by considering the logical merits of the arguments and models that have led other writers to expect that small nations may be affected similarly by events such as devaluation or membership in a customs union and then in each case marshal what evidence is available to confirm or refute the relevance of these models to our group of small developed countries.

CHAPTER III

Small Nations—Are They Unstable or Dependent?

I

It has been stated many times that small nations are "dependent" on international trade, although the term "trade dependence" is used with a diversity of connotations. Some writers have suggested that dependence on international trade be measured by the ratio of exports of goods and services to national product,[1] which states the share of national incomes received that is generated in the export sector, if one disregards the import content of exports. On the other hand, the ratio of imports to national product as a measure of "import dependence" approximates the extent of reliance of aggregate expenditure on foreign sources for consumer and capital goods.[2] We have already examined evidence relating to the combined trade ratio in the previous chapter.

It has also been suggested that imports are more "essential" per unit to small nations than they are to large nations in the sense that the opportunity cost of domestic production of imports relative to the cost of acquiring them through international trade will generally be higher in small nations. The Graham model in Chapter VI does indicate that small nations tend to enjoy greater gains per unit of trade to the extent that they specialize in only one or a few goods in which they enjoy a great comparative advantage. However, not every small country is so fortunate. (This same tendency applies to developing or "poor" countries which are also small in the relevant sense of productive capacity.) Furthermore, the question how to measure the gains from trade still defies the best efforts of international trade specialists.

A meaningful and measurable alternative notion of "essentiality" is the import coefficient of an industry or of an aggregate of expenditure such as total consumption or total investment. Direct, or preferably direct plus indirect, Leontief coefficients give a crude idea of the

---

1. For example, Triffin, in *Economic Consequences*, p. 394.
2. See, for example, H. H. Leisner, *The Import Dependence of Britain and West Germany*, Princeton Studies in International Finance, No. 7 (Princeton, 1957).

importance of imported inputs to major producing sectors or aggregates of expenditure. The average import content of gross domestic capital formation for a group of small developed countries was recently estimated by Kuznets at 49–52 per cent, and for small developing countries it was 41–69 per cent. These estimates compare with 17 per cent for large developed countries and 29 per cent for large developing countries.[3] In all groups the direct import content of consumption was less than 30 per cent.[4] In Table III-1 below the approximate direct import content of consumption expenditure and of capital formation for the fifteen countries is derived by multiplying the ratio of imports to gross domestic product by the proportion of consumption and capital goods respectively in total imports and dividing by the consumption and capital formation share of gross domestic product. These calculations of import content are indirect and understate the true proportions somewhat because two commodity groups of imports, "Fuel" and "Unallocated," have not been allocated to either consumption or investment. Nevertheless, the much smaller proportion of consumption expenditure devoted to imports compared with investment is true of every country. If one were to add indirect import requirements for local production of producer goods, as in input-output analyses, the import coefficient of investment would be higher.

It is evident that capital formation in small developed countries, even the industrialized European countries, is very dependent on imports of fixed capital goods or their components. In Chenery's study of industrial growth, the industries having significant size elasticities or "economies of scale" include Metals, Machinery, Transport Equipment, and Chemicals.[5] This conjuncture of evidence supports the frequent claim that small countries have difficulty in producing durable capital-intensive products and especially fixed capital goods because of large economies of scale in these industries and must therefore import the bulk of their requirements of these products. This form of dependence on imports of fixed capital goods has lately received a great deal of attention in discussions of the "trade gap" constraint on economic growth in developing countries. It seems that all small developed countries unable to produce much of their own specialized fixed capital

---

3. Kuznets, "Level and Structure of Foreign Trade," Table 17, ll. 19, 21.
4. Maizels, *Industrial Growth and World Trade*, chap. vi, finds size of country (in terms of population) to be a statistically significant determinant of the import content of aggregate consumption.
5. "Patterns of Industrial Growth," pp. 645–646. See chap. vii, sec. iii, below, for a brief discussion of the empirical evidence concerning economies of scale.

Table III-1 DIRECT IMPORTS IN CONSUMPTION AND CAPITAL FORMATION, 1960 (percentages)

Country	Ratio of total imports to GDP (1)	Ratio of total consumption to GDP (2)	Ratio of fixed capital formation to GDP (3)	Ratio of consumption goods imports to total imports (4)
Australia	18	76	25	50.8
Netherlands	48	70	24	47.3
Sweden	28	77	22	44.7
Belgium-Luxembourg	36	81	19	54.4
South Africa	25	77	20	54.0
Switzerland	29	72	23	55.3
Denmark	34	79	19	50.6
Austria	26	73	24	54.0
Norway	43	72	29	35.1
Venezuela	21	76	20	38.4
New Zealand	26	79	23	52.4
Finland	24	70	27	42.7
Israel	35	92	26	52.2
Ireland	36	87	14	53.4
Puerto Rico	60	94	20	N.A.

Table III-1 (cont.)

Country	Ratio of producer durable goods to total imports (5)	Ratio of imported consumption goods to total consumption Col. (1) × Col. (4) / Col. (2)	Ratio of imported durable producer goods to gross domestic capital formation Col. (1) × Col. (5) / Col. (3)
Australia	32.6	12.0	23.5
Netherlands	31.4	32.4	62.9
Sweden	33.4	16.2	42.5
Belgium-Luxembourg	30.7	24.2	58.2
South Africa	34.8	17.5	43.5
Switzerland	31.1	22.3	39.2
Denmark	29.1	21.8	52.1
Austria	32.4	19.2	35.1
Norway	50.4	21.0	74.8
Venezuela	48.9	10.6	51.4
New Zealand	48.4	17.2	54.7
Finland	28.7	14.6	25.5
Israel	36.3	20.0	48.9
Ireland	22.5	22.1	57.9
Puerto Rico	N.A.	N.A.	N.A.

Sources: Cols. (1) through (3): United Nations *Yearbook of National Accounts Statistics,* 1964. Total consumption is private plus government consumption. These columns relate to 1960. Cols. (4) and (5): Kuznets, "Level and Structure of Foreign Trade," Appendix Table 7. Consumer goods include all raw and semifabricated materials to be made into finished consumer goods; producer goods include finished equipment and unfinished raw and semifabricated materials to be made into finished producer goods. For most countries these ratios are averages for 1957–1960.

goods requirements are vulnerable to this "trade gap" in the same way as developing countries.[6]

The above concepts of dependence have all been concerned with the role of trade in determining the level of current real income. Dependence is often related instead to the frequency and amplitude of fluctuations in real income that come about through fluctuations in the trade sector. Discussion of "trade dependence" over the last thirty years in Australia and New Zealand, for example, has been preoccupied with the instability of real income.[7] This question of instability of incomes arising in the foreign trade sector will be deferred until Section II.

Still other concepts of dependence occur. An Australian economist, T. W. Swan, defined a dependent economy as "a small country which trades in world markets that are competitive in the sense that the prices it receives and pays for imports are independent of its domestic conditions of supply and demand."[8] That is, it is a price-taker; its export and import prices and terms of trade are given. The belief that small nations have a highly elastic foreign demand for their exports is important in the context of a possible devaluation (see Chapter V). To be a price-taker requires that a country account for only a very small share of the total sales in foreign markets for each of its export products. Do small countries typically conform to this pattern? It is true that the total export receipts of each of the fifteen small developed countries comprise less than 4 per cent of total world exports.[9] Since total world exports are a minimum estimate of the foreign market for all internationally-traded products, their shares of all foreign markets are even smaller. But this fact is offset by the tendency of these countries, and of all countries, to concentrate their actual exports on a few commodities, exporting no amounts of many important traded commodities. Hence the presumption that their share of individual markets is small is no longer certain.

This is particularly true of small countries exporting primary products. In 1963, according to International Monetary Fund statistics,

---

6. In one of the earliest formulations of the trade gap idea Chenery and Bruno were concerned with Israel; Hollis B. Chenery and M. Bruno, "Development Alternatives in an Open Economy: The Case of Israel," *Economic Journal*, LXXII (March, 1962), 79–103.

7. Horace Belshaw, "Stabilisation in a Dependent Economy," *Economic Record*, XV (April, 1939), 40–58; C. G. F. Simkin, *The Instability of a Dependent Economy* (Oxford, 1951); T. W. Swan, "Economic Control in a Dependent Economy," *Economic Record*, XXXVI (March, 1960), 51–66.

8. Swan, "Economic Control in a Dependent Economy," p. 53.

9. Appendix II and United Nations, *Yearbook of International Trade Statistics*, 1964.

Australian staple exports of wool, sugar, wheat, hides, and lead amounted to 54, 13, 13, 19, and 36 per cent, respectively, of total world exports of these commodities. New Zealand's exports of wool, lamb, and butter were 17, 72, and 33 per cent, respectively, of world trade. Denmark's butter trade constituted 24 per cent of the world total and its bacon 94 per cent, while Sweden and Finland between them supplied over one-half the total world trade in newsprint and pulp.[1]

Michael Michaely made a bold attempt to measure the extent to which forty-four countries occupied a large or small share in the markets of their major exports during 1954.[2] He developed an index, W_{jx}, called the "commodity-weighted share of world exports." For each country this index is defined as $100 \sum_{i=1}^{n} \left[\frac{X_{ij}}{X_j} \cdot \frac{X_{ij}}{X_i} \right]$ where X_{ij} is the country's exports of commodity i, X_j is the value of its total exports, and X_i total world exports of the commodity i. Thus this index sums the shares of the country's exports in total world trade for each of n internationally-traded commodities, weighting each world share by the share of this commodity in the country's total export trade. It is the appropriate measure in this context. By a simple transformation,

$$W_{jx} = 100 \, X_j \cdot \sum_{i=1}^{n} \left[\frac{1}{X_i} \left(\frac{X_{ij}}{X_j} \right)^2 \right].$$

A commodity-weighted share is the smaller the smaller the country's total export trade, the larger the world trade in the commodities it exports, and the less concentrated its export trade as measured by the Hirschman Index of concentration, $100 \sqrt{\sum_{i=1}^{n} \left(\frac{X_{ij}}{X_j} \right)^2}.$

Michaely's results are very revealing. The extent to which higher commodity concentration in some small countries offsets their small shares of world export trade is such that "the larger trading countries have, on the average, practically the same commodity-weighted share in world trade as all the rest, save the smallest trading countries. . . . many of the smaller economies have a stronger monopolistic position, in this sense, than most of the large countries."[3] Michaely used population as the criterion of national size. Yet, the small countries considered in this book for which Michaely calculated commodity-

---

1. International Monetary Fund, *International Financial Statistics* (July, 1966), pp. 26–28.
2. *Concentration in International Trade*, chap. iii.
3. *Ibid.*, pp. 35, 59.

weighted shares ranked as follows: Australia (6), Denmark (9), Ireland (15), Finland (18), Sweden (20), Belgium-Luxembourg (24), Netherlands (26), Norway (29), Austria (35). The actual value of these shares ranged from 25.0 per cent for Australia to 5.5 per cent for Austria. The high ranking of Australia and Denmark in particular demonstrates once again the importance of these countries in the markets of their major exports. These statistics conclusively refute the notion that the export sales of small countries comprise a small share of foreign markets and that therefore small countries are price-takers in their export markets. We shall use this conclusion in the discussion of devaluation in Chapter V.

Finally, if one takes a longer-run view, a country may be dependent on other countries for one or more elements necessary to economic growth: supplies of unskilled, skilled, or entrepreneurial labor; markets; innovations; overseas savings; or other elements. The size of nations has received very scant attention as a determinant of the rate of economic growth. The two papers presented at the Lisbon conference by Kuznets and by Leduc and Weiller were, to the author's knowledge, the first to ponder possible ways in which national size may affect the process of economic growth. Not unexpectedly, the emphasis in both of these papers was on the supposed tendency of small nations to have high trade ratios and a highly concentrated export trade and the dangers these characteristics may pose for the long-run rate of growth. They feared that reliance on a few exports as the "engine of growth" may cause the secular rate of growth in small nations to be uneven, and possibly slower.[4] (This is essentially the same line of argument as the one concerning developing countries which export primary products.) Size of countries could affect the rate of growth in other ways. Large economies of scale may restrict the choice of industries and the pattern of industrial growth in small countries.[5] Rising costs and technical complexities may handicap small nations in making and adapting innovations.[6]

In favor of small nations, an argument has been made that small countries may be more adaptable than large countries because the governments of small culturally homogeneous societies may be able to

---

4. *Economic Consequences*, pp. 208–210, 382.
5. *Ibid.*, especially papers by Jewkes ("Are the Economies of Scale Unlimited?"), Edwards, and V. A. Marsan ("The Experience of Italy"). For a statistical analysis, see Chenery, "Patterns of Industrial Growth," pp. 645–646. Also Demas, *Economics of Development in Small Countries*, chap. ii.
6. *Economics of Development in Small Countries*, pp. 109–113, 157–159. Balassa, *Theory of Economic Integration*, pp. 159, 174–175, enumerates the advantages of a larger market for making innovation.

act more rapidly and effectively.⁷ The small size of their gross domestic products construes a second advantage in that it has enabled some small countries to borrow amounts of overseas capital that form a large proportion of their national products and total imports. According to Kuznets, over the period 1957–1961 the current account deficits plus net transfers were, as a percentage of gross national product, Israel (22.5), Puerto Rico (19.1), Ireland (3.7), Norway (2.9), Australia (2.7), and New Zealand (1.9). These deficits plus net transfers financed from 58 per cent of total imports in the case of Israel to 6.6 per cent for Norway.⁸ On the other hand, the small Continental European countries and South Africa and Venezuela lent substantial proportions of their gross national products to other nations.

In each of these suggestions the connection between size of nations and the rate of growth is rather tenuous. The determinants of the rate of growth of any country are numerous, interdependent, and complex. It is not possible here to conduct any extensive investigation into the principal causes of differential rates of growth. I shall merely note that for developed European and North American countries alone there does not appear to be any association between the size of the country and the ex post rate of growth. A major study carried out by the Economic Commission for Europe calculated rates of growth in European and North American countries for the decade of the fifties.⁹ The report shows trend rates, eliminating the influences of boom or recession in the terminal years. The results are cited in Table III-2. During this period Austria, Switzerland, and the Netherlands had relatively high average rates of growth of real gross domestic product, all in excess of 5 per cent, but Denmark, Belgium, and Ireland kept company with the United Kingdom at the bottom of the scale. The Austrian and Finnish achievements are noteworthy because both economies suffered substantial dislocation after World War II. Of the non-European small countries, Israel has had since its inception one of the most spectacular growth rates of all nations, despite its political troubles. Though the data for the forty-year period, 1913–1956, are less reliable, Switzerland and Finland almost matched the fastest growing countries, the United States and Canada, but Ireland, Austria, and Belgium were among the laggards. It is conceivable but unlikely,

---

7. *Economic Consequences*, pp. 28–32, 208–209, 382–383; Demas, *Economics of Development in Small Countries*, pp. 81–82.

8. "Level and Structure of Foreign Trade," Appendix Table 8 and pp. 71–77; *Economic Consequences*, p. 23. For an account of the extreme Israeli experience as a capital importer, see S. Riemer, "Israel: Ten Years of Economic Dependence," *Oxford Economic Papers*, XII (June, 1960), 141–169.

9. *Some Factors in Economic Growth in Europe during the 1950's* (Geneva, 1964).

in view of the complexity of the determinants of economic growth and

Table III-2 RATES OF GROWTH OF SMALL AND LARGE EUROPEAN AND NORTH AMERICAN COUNTRIES (percentages)

Country	1949–1959 Average trend rates of growth		1913–1956 Average rate of growth of GDP
	GDP	GDP per capita	
West Germany	7.4	6.3	2.1
Austria	6.0	5.8	1.4
Iceland	5.4	3.2	N.A.
Switzerland	5.2	3.8	3.1
Netherlands	4.8	3.5	2.6
France	4.5	3.6	1.3
Canada	4.2	1.5	3.2
Finland	4.2	3.1	3.1
Luxembourg	3.8	3.2	N.A.
Norway	3.4	2.5	3.0
Sweden	3.4	2.8	2.4
United States	3.3	1.5	3.2
Denmark	3.2	2.4	2.2
Belgium	3.0	2.4	1.6
United Kingdom	2.4	2.0	1.6
Ireland	1.3	1.8	1.3

Source: Economic Commission for Europe, *Some Factors in Economic Growth in Europe during the 1950's,* chap. ii, Tables 1 and 2. Iceland's rates of growth are actual instead of trend rates.

their indirect connections with country size, that a multi-variable analysis could find some general statistical relationship between the rate of growth and the size of nations.

Small nations may or may not be particularly dependent on international trade in the above senses. The idea of trade dependence is subject to several widely differing interpretations, and it seems more fruitful to move on to the more clearly defined issue of whether small nations are more unstable than large nations.

II

Discussions of instability often embrace both short-term instability due to cyclical and non-cyclical changes in market conditions and instability in the rate of economic growth over longer periods. The latter type of long-run instability lies outside the scope of this study, and in any case there are insufficient reliable data to reach any conclusions.

The marketing of all commodities is subject to risks because of imperfect knowledge and unpredictable changes in demand and production conditions. Commodities sold at home are subject to these normal risks just as are the commodities exported. However, most writers on international trade emphasize that there are additional, "special" risks attached to selling goods in foreign markets. Not only do exporters face tariffs, quotas, and other forms of protection abroad, but the level of these restrictions is subject to alteration at all times. Similarly, production for a market in a different currency area involves risks of changes in currency convertibility, the exchange rate, or other currency restrictions. For these reasons the markets for individual export goods may be more risky and subject to more frequent and greater fluctuations than those for commodities produced and marketed domestically, especially non-tradable commodities not subject to any foreign competition. The second important feature distinguishing disturbances in the foreign trade sector from those in the non-trade sectors is that the former are "autonomous" in the sense that they are largely beyond the control of the home country.

If one accepts that the sales of export products are in fact somewhat more liable to fluctuations than sales of domestic products, then it follows that a high ratio of exports of goods and services to national product will increase the probability of fluctuations in income for the whole economy, other things being equal. But other things are not equal; as is noted later in this section, the ratio of X/Y is by no means the sole or even the main factor determining the extent of income instability due to changes in export income. (There is another and quite different side to the relationship between the trade sector and non-trade sectors. A large trade sector may dampen down fluctuations originating in domestic expenditures via change in import expenditure and its effects on the cash balances of individual consumers and the banking system.)

Moreover, the extent of short-term fluctuations in the economy as a whole depends on the extent of "autonomous" change in the foreign trade sector and in the non-trade sectors, the multiplier processes, interaction among trade and non-trade sectors, the reactions of the fiscal and monetary authorities, and other factors. We should not be surprised if there is no correspondence between fluctuations in national income or other national aggregates on the one hand and the size of the country on the other; what evidence has been collected suggests there is little correspondence.[1] It is a common observation

---

1. L. Tarshis, in *Economic Consequences*, pp. 190–199; *ibid.*, pp. 387–394; Economic Commission for Europe, *Some Factors in Economic Growth in Europe,* chap. ii, chart i.

that several small countries—for example, Sweden—were less severely affected by the Great Depression than were such large countries as the United States and Germany.[2]

Rather than attempt a cross-country analysis of all causes of instability of national income or other economy-wide variables, I shall confine my attention to instability in the trade sector alone. Since the degrees of cyclical and non-cyclical short-run fluctuations originating in the foreign trade sector will be affected by much the same set of factors, they will be considered together. To be exact, by instability in this sector is meant the year-to-year changes in export receipts from the sale of goods and services, corrected for the trend. All capital transactions and their many repercussions on capital formation and the balance of payments are ignored. Export receipts are the best variable in considering the effects on the rest of the economy of instability arising in the trade sector. A major incidental advantage in this definition of the problem is that it allows the use of the results of Joseph Coppock's exhaustive study of the causes of international economic instability in the post-World War II period.[3]

What are the possible major factors explaining fluctuations in export income alone, and what is their connection, if any, with the size of nations? First, the higher the degree of geographic concentration in a country's export trade, the more liable are its export receipts to fluctuations originating in changes in the level of imports or a devaluation or other events in its *major market or markets*. Table III-3 shows the extent to which the national products of the fifteen small nations are derived from sales to one country. These ratios are approximate because the shares of the largest market in total exports refer to commodity trade alone. The share of exports of goods plus services was not available in many countries. In those countries where the share of the largest partner in merchandise exports exceeds its share in total exports of both goods and services, the ratio of the largest market's merchandise sales to national product overstates the true importance to national product of the largest foreign market. This source of error is believed to be small since merchandise exports make up 80 per cent or more of total exports in most countries, and for most nations the same country is dominant in service exports and in commodity exports. The export trade of each of these small countries with their largest partner varies widely as a share of gross domestic product. The four countries which derive more than 10 per cent

---

2. *Economic Consequences*, pp. 70–71, 190.
3. *International Economic Instability*.

Table III-3 APPROXIMATE RATIO OF LARGEST EXPORT MARKET TO GROSS DOMESTIC PRODUCT, 1964 (percentages)

Country	Ratio of exports of goods and services to GDP (1)	Share of largest market in total exports (2)	Ratio of largest market in GDP (1) × (2)
Australia	16	18.3	2.9
Netherlands	46	26.9	12.4
Sweden	26	14.3	3.7
Belgium-Luxembourg	38	22.9	8.7
South Africa	27	16.3	4.4
Switzerland	29	31.5	9.1
Denmark	31	23.1	7.2
Austria	26	27.9	7.3
Norway	42	20.1	8.4
Venezuela	36	33.9	12.2
New Zealand	24	49.5	11.9
Finland	21	22.4	4.7
Israel	22	14.5	3.2
Ireland	31	72.0	22.3
Puerto Rico	45	N.A.	N.A.

Sources: Col. (1) from United Nations, *Yearbook of National Accounts Statistics,* 1965. Col. (2) from Table II-2.

of GDP from one foreign market are marked by either a particularly high ratio of X/GDP (Netherlands), or a high geographic concentration in one market (New Zealand), or both (Ireland and Venezuela).

However, a high geographic concentration of exports in one or a few markets need not increase the probability of instability of *total* export receipts. This probability depends on the relative stability of imports of goods and services in the countries to which exports are directed. Import instability varies greatly from country to country as Coppock's calculations reveal.[4] All the small countries listed in Table III-3, with the sole exception of Belgium-Luxembourg, sent the largest share of their exports to the United Kingdom, the United States, or West Germany, and the total imports of these three countries are among the world's most stable. Contrary to popular belief, Coppock in his study of the export instability of eighty-three countries finds that "regional concentration of export destination, measured in three different ways, was the characteristic most closely associated with *stability* of exports."[5] Nevertheless, as was noted in the previous chapter, there are dangers in geographic dependence on one large foreign market in

---
4. *Ibid.,* p. 85.
5. *Ibid.,* p. 139. Italics mine.

the event of a major upheaval in this market, resulting perhaps from that nation's joining a customs union, a declaration of war, or some other major event. Hirschman, in his pioneer analysis of the trading relations among large and small nations, particularly the exploitation by Nazi Germany of her small mid-European suppliers during the thirties, provides a fascinating account of the exercise of "national power" by a large nation over small nations. He suggests that a small nation, in order to protect itself from the manipulations of a powerful trading partner, will have a certain maximum limit to the total amount of trade it may safely conduct with that country.[6]

There is an even more widespread conviction that a high degree of commodity concentration of exports increases the instability of export receipts. This familiar notion is widespread in many developing countries as well as in some small countries. According to this view we should expect a positive correlation between commodity concentration and instability of export receipts. Coppock tests this hypothesis.[7] His simple correlation coefficient between export instability and the Hirschman Index of commodity concentration, apparently based on the two-digit SITC groups, is very low (.04) and quite insignificant. His measure of instability is the logarithmic variance, corrected for trend, for the years 1946–1958. The relationship between these two variables does not show up any better in the multiple correlation analysis. A weak association appears when all countries are grouped into three very broad groups.

In his analysis of the causes of year-to-year fluctuation in export *prices*—which coincidentally covers almost exactly the same time period as that of Coppock—Michael Michaely finds that "this causal relationship between commodity concentration and price fluctuations of exports does exist, but that it is not strong."[8] One interesting feature of Michaely's results is the tendency for the range of the degree of fluctuations to splay out as the degree of commodity concentration increases, which suggests that a parabolic regression could be fitted. With higher concentration the nature of the commodity becomes very important. Those countries which specialize in the "wrong" export goods—those having prices which tend to fluctuate greatly—have a high degree of fluctuation, while those who concentrate on exporting

---

6. *National Power*, p. 19. Small nations should also avoid monopolistic devices employed by large importers of their goods to strengthen their dependence on these large countries. These include various devices deliberately employed to drive their export prices above ruling world prices (chap. ii). See also Duncan, "The Small State and International Economic Equilibrium," for similar views.
7. *International Economic Instability*, chaps. v and vi.
8. *Concentration in International Trade*, p. 72.

the "right" commodities—those with stable prices—have a low degree of fluctuation. Thus concentration may be important in that for countries which export principally either "right" or "wrong" commodities, it accentuates the "rightness" or "wrongness" of their exports and accordingly produces an unusually low or high degree of price fluctuation. Which are right or wrong commodities? There is a familiar contention that on the average the prices of primary products tend to fluctuate more than those of manufactures. The export prices of countries exporting principally primary products are therefore said to fluctuate more than those specializing in manufactures. Both these fond notions are shattered by the statistics, though there is evidence that the variation among individual primary products is greater than among individual manufactured products.[9] We should also remember that variations in the quantity of exports do partially offset variations in prices, and in Coppock's study of the postwar period the quantity variations are clearly the more important.

Coppock included national income and per capita incomes among the twelve independent variables he tested in his multiple correlation analysis. Neither size as measured by national income nor the level of development were significant determinants of export fluctuations. Indeed, no variable other than the quantity of exports proved to have a consistent influence. "The analysis shows that high instability is associated with various combinations of characteristics. We should not be too surprised at this result. A phenomenon can be the resultant of various combinations of variable forces." [1]

Table III-4 lists Coppock's index of export instability for the fifteen small developed nations. As one would expect from the above conclusions, there is quite a variation among the countries in the degree of instability of export receipts which they have experienced, though all but two have below average instability. Nor is there any apparent relation with the extent of commodity concentration of exports. My 1964 indices are also listed, since these are based on the three-digit SITC classes rather than the two-digit groups as in Coppock's study; consequently they show a much greater dispersion. The explanation for the two most unstable countries, Finland and Australia, is that each specializes heavily in one product—pulp and paper and wool, respectively—the prices for which show among the greatest annual variation for all primary products,[2] even though the indices of commodity concentration for the two countries are lower than average.

9. *Ibid.*, pp. 75–81; Coppock, *International Economic Instability*, pp. 42–47, 103.
1. Coppock, *International Economic Instability*, p. 139.
2. *Ibid.*, p. 43, Table 3–6.

At the other end of the scale, Switzerland and Ireland were actually the two most stable of all the eighty-three countries in the Coppock list.[3]

One author at the 1957 Lisbon conference ventured the opinion that "because of their smaller size relative to world markets, and the shorter lines of internal communication, these small countries can

Table III-4 INSTABILITY OF ANNUAL EXPORT RECEIPTS IN SMALL COUNTRIES, 1946–1958

Country	Coppock's index of export instability 1946–1958	Coppock's index of commodity concentration 1957	Index of commodity concentration 1964
Australia	24.6	65.5	36.69
Netherlands	21.4	47.3	9.60
Sweden	15.1	56.1	17.82
Belgium-Luxembourg	18.5	65.7	11.37
South Africa	N.A.	N.A.	19.14
Switzerland	6.2	61.6	18.32
Denmark	10.0	66.4	15.66
Austria	21.4	60.8	10.81
Norway	16.4	87.0	16.77
Venezuela	16.1	92.1	70.72
New Zealand	14.7	69.3	43.83
Finland	30.4	60.8	38.07
Israel	12.0	60.1	40.65
Ireland	6.3	70.6	30.64
Puerto Rico	9.2	N.A.	N.A.
Mean—all countries	21.8	69.6	42.6
Standard deviation	11.5	14.0	

Sources: Cols. (1) and (2): Coppock, *International Economic Instability*, Appendix Table A.2. Col. (3): Table II-2, above. The mean and standard deviations in Cols. (1) and (2) refer to all eighty-three countries.

adjust more rapidly to changing conditions."[4] Others observed that firms in small nations tend to be less specialized, each plant producing a diversity of products, a characterization which fits the Swiss case well.[5] However, as I. Svennilson insisted at that time, the success of some small countries such as Switzerland and Belgium in overcoming the inherent instability of their vital export markets does not demonstrate the greater flexibility of small nations in general.[6] All it shows

---

3. *Ibid.*, p. 50.
4. Kuznets, in *Economic Consequences*, p. 30. Cf. Tarshis, in *ibid.*, p. 198, and Leduc and Weiller, in *ibid.*, p. 209.
5. *Ibid.*, pp. 124–125, 370–371, and for an account of Swiss experience in this respect, pp. 70–71. Curiously, Coppock makes a similar suggestion, *International Economic Instability*, p. 105.
6. *Economic Consequences*, p. 352.

is that these successful small nations have been forced to make such changes in order to succeed.

Looking at all eight-three countries, the fifteen small nations are distributed throughout the list when they are ranked in order of their export instability over the twenty-two years. It is the specific circumstances of each country with respect to the kind of commodities exported, access to markets over the period of years, commodity concentration, adaptability to changes in market conditions, and numerous other factors—rather than country size or any other single variable—which must be used to explain the pattern of export instability.

Some policy implications of these conclusions should be noted. Deliberate diversification of the commodities exported is not likely to reduce the fluctuations in export receipts unless a country diversifies along the "right" lines; that is, unless it develops new commodity exports for which receipts (rather than prices) are more stable than those of existing exports. In view of the importance of such factors as location, degree of industrial development, and access to markets, development of new exports is not easy. We can presume that most countries whose exports are highly concentrated in a few commodities are this way because of the absence of other potential exports which could be developed readily. And the degree of stability of commodities in the past may not be a good guide to future stability in a rapidly changing world. Fundamentally, as Coppock noted, it is clear that "measures to cushion countries against the shock of changes in their export earnings are much more feasible than measures to maintain export earnings." [7] Finally, prospects for growth of total receipts may be as important as stability of these receipts.

No generalizations concerning instability in the trade sector are applicable to small countries generally. Moreover, the severity of changes in total domestic expenditure and income induced by changes in the *export* sector will also depend on the mechanism by which autonomous changes in exports are transmitted through the whole economy. The theory of foreign trade multipliers enables one, under certain assumptions, to predict the effect of changes in autonomous components of expenditure on total income and expenditure. In general, the higher the import propensities and the lower the foreign repercussions, the lower will be the value of these multipliers. Investment expenditure and the expenditure of central governments on goods and services may be linked to export income by such factors as the level of profits, taxation revenues, and the level of confidence

---

7. Coppock, *International Economic Instability*, p. 155.

if for example an export boom is expected, perhaps optimistically, to continue. These factors can greatly increase the destabilizing effect of export fluctuations. In the next chapter we consider whether the operation of foreign trade multipliers in small countries differs from that in large countries.

CHAPTER IV

Foreign Trade Multipliers and the Balance of Payments in Small Nations

I

The theory of foreign trade multipliers shows one mechanism by which an initial expansion or contraction in expenditure in one country interacts with the level of expenditure in countries with which it trades to determine short-run changes in the incomes of these countries. This chapter seeks to discover how the factor of national size affects the operation of foreign trade multipliers. It will be seen that national size does have important implications for the effect of fluctuations of export and other income on balance of payments stability in particular. The practical importance of these implications for some small nations is illustrated by the example of an export boom in the New Zealand economy in 1963–1964 and the unusual behavior of that country's balance of payments. This analysis is intended to apply to small developed rather than to small developing nations. Some national income models relating to developing countries are similar in certain respects to the one below, but others have stressed different peculiarities of certain developing countries.[1]

Consider one country, called the "home country," whose autonomous expenditure on its own products is assumed to increase, as a result, for example, of an increase in government or investment expenditure. The greater the marginal propensity to import, the smaller the value of the multiplier for a given value of the home country's marginal propensity to absorb its own products. The effect of a high marginal

---

1. H. C. Wallich, "Underdeveloped Countries and the International Monetary Mechanism," in *Money, Trade and Economic Growth: Essays in Honor of John H. Williams* (New York, 1951), pp. 15–32, suggested that in an export economy selling primary products abroad, both government and investment expenditure are highly dependent on export receipts and that an export boom could have much the same type of destabilizing effect as is described in this chapter. Clark W. Reynolds, "Domestic Consequences of Export Instability," *American Economic Review*, LIII (May, 1963), 93–102, proposes a similar model. On the other hand, Jonathan V. Levin, *The Export Economies* (Cambridge, Mass., 1960), argues that until recently at least export earnings in export economies had no internal foreign multiplier effects since a large part of these earnings were remitted abroad directly as foreign profits or earnings of emigrant labor and little of that left in the country was spent on locally produced goods (pp. 193–202).

propensity to import is like that of a high marginal propensity to save; it dampens the multiplying effect of the initial autonomous increase in expenditure and has a stabilizing effect on national income.

This import effect must be modified when the repercussions of income movements in the home country on the income and expenditure of the trading partner countries are taken into account. An increase in the imports of the home country results in an increase in the exports of its trading partners, which in turn leads to an increase in the national incomes of its trading partners, and to an increase in their imports, some part of which will normally be obtained from the home country itself. Hence the original increase in the imports of the home country ultimately leads to some "foreign repercussions" or "backwash" increase in the foreign demand for its own exports.

Two characteristics of small countries are supposed to affect the value of this multiplier in these countries. First, it is commonly stated in the discussion of foreign trade multipliers, as in other connections discussed in this book, that small countries tend to have high ratios of imports to national income; that is, a high average propensity to import. It is therefore presumed that they will have a high marginal propensity to import.[2] Unfortunately, no direct estimates of the marginal propensities are available. The 1964 trade statistics for the fifteen small developed countries confirm the high ratios of imports to domestic product of these countries; they ranged from a low of 18 per cent (Australia) to a high of 67 per cent (Puerto Rico).[3] By contrast, the average propensities to import of large developed countries are relatively low. The statistics of trade ratios in Chapter II showed all countries whose gross domestic products exceeded $20 billion to have below average trade ratios. Their ratios of imports of goods and services to gross domestic product are even lower in relation to other countries than their total trade ratios since most large developed countries have annual export surpluses. For example, the import ratios of France, the United States, and West Germany in 1964 were 14, 4, and 18 per cent, respectively.[4] One may presume that small specialized countries depending on imports for a wide range of consumer and capital goods in particular, generally do have high marginal propen-

---

2. William A. Salant, "Foreign Trade Policy," pp. 213–215. See also Fritz Machlup, *International Trade and the National Income Multiplier* (Philadelphia, 1943), pp. 201–202, and Charles P. Kindleberger, *International Economics* (2nd ed.; Homewood, Ill., 1958), pp. 173–174.
3. United Nations, *Yearbook of National Accounts Statistics*, 1965, Table 3.
4. *Ibid.*

sities to import in addition to high average propensities to import, relative to the large developed countries.

Second, it is argued that the "foreign repercussions" are not significant in small countries.[5] William A. Salant appears to have been the first to contend that one determinant of the magnitude of these repercussions is the size of the home country in terms of the total value of its export trade. Indeed, he defines a small economy as one which has a high average propensity to import (and presumably a high marginal propensity to import), and whose exports constitute a small fraction of total world exports.[6] This definition of a small country introduces smallness directly into the theory of foreign trade multipliers. I shall, however, continue to use the definition of size in terms of national income, but I shall assume that small countries have these associated characteristics. This is true of the fifteen selected small countries. I have already commented on these countries in regard to their marginal propensities to import, and their shares in total world export trade are certainly very small. In fact, for 1964 the largest share in world exports for any of these countries was that of the Netherlands at 3.4 per cent.[7]

An induced increase in imports of one of these small countries whose autonomous expenditure increases is thus large in relation to its national income, but small relative to the incomes of the other countries of the world. Although the increase in its imports leads to some change in the incomes of its trading partners and, therefore, their total imports, this change was not thought likely to lead to a significant secondary increase in demand for the small country's exports since the latter has only a very small share of total world exports. On the other hand, a large country's small marginal propensity to import does not greatly dampen the income effects of an initial autonomous change in its expenditure. Moreover, for a large country the "foreign repercussions" may be quite significant, because the increase in the imports of a large country, though small in relation to its own income, may represent a substantial increase in the income of some foreign countries. The relatively small marginal propensity to import and the larger "foreign repercussions" led Salant and Machlup to expect that the value of the foreign trade multiplier for a given auton-

---

5. Salant, "Foreign Trade Policy," p. 214; Kindleberger, *International Economics*, p. 188; Machlup, *International Trade*, p. 201.
6. Salant, "Foreign Trade Policy," p. 214.
7. Calculated from United Nations, *Yearbook of International Trade Statistics*, 1965, Table 3.

omous change in the home country's expenditure will be somewhat greater in large countries than in small countries. The same conclusion could be transferred to other multipliers which state the change in a country's income when autonomous expenditures in foreign countries are assumed to have changed, since these other multipliers are also partly determined, in different ways, by the import propensity of the country and the foreign repercussions which follow any change in its income.

However, as we shall see, foreign repercussions do not depend directly upon a country's share of world exports, except under special assumptions. Under certain strict symmetry assumptions first explored by Fritz Machlup, it is always true that the larger the country in a given international trade setting, the larger the value of its foreign trade multipliers. This case is explored in the Appendix, not so much because of its conclusion which is intuitively obvious, but because of the interesting manner of introducing country size as a variable. But, in general, Machlup showed that if each of a group of countries has a different marginal propensity to import goods from the one home country being considered, the outcome of an autonomous change in the home country's expenditure will depend on the distribution among foreign countries of the home country's import trade.[8]

In order to predict more accurately the final change in national income of a country for a given initial change in a world of many countries, one must investigate the behavior of the n-country matrix multipliers developed simultaneously by Lloyd Metzler and John S. Chipman in 1950.[9] These matrix multipliers take account of the induced imports from all foreign countries and also the secondary repercussions on each country's income via changes in the income and imports of its trading partners. In the following multi-country model, the final change in the incomes of each country following a change in expenditure in one country will be seen to depend in a complex way on the values, in all countries, of the marginal propensities to absorb own products and the marginal propensities to import goods from each of the trading partners.

II

I have yet to spell out the model which yields these results. All func-

---

8. *International Trade*, pp. 90–92.
9. Lloyd Metzler, "A Multi-Region Theory of Income and Trade," *Econometrica*, XVIII (Oct., 1950), 329–354, and John S. Chipman, "The Multi-Sector Multiplier," *Econometrica*, XVIII (Oct., 1950), 355–374. See also John S. Chipman, "The Theory of Inter-Sectoral Money Flows and Income Formation," *Johns Hopkins University Studies in Historical and Political Science*, LXVIII, No. 2 (1950), 1–155. This chapter is principally an adaptation of their matrix multipliers.

tional relationships are expressed in terms of current money values since we wish to note the effects of changes on the balance of payments as well as on national incomes. If all prices, including the exchange rates, were held constant, all changes in national incomes and expenditures would also be changes in real magnitudes. Instead, it is assumed here that the aggregate supply curve may be less than perfectly price-elastic; thus part of any increase in current national incomes may represent rising price levels. The continuous increases in current national incomes possible in this model imply a permissive attitude on the part of monetary authorities. The money sector is not explicitly treated, following the procedure of almost all foreign trade multiplier models, and I have abstracted from such things as real-balance effects and the restraint rising interest rates have on investment. The results are consistent with a "neutral" monetary policy that maintains an infinitely elastic supply of money and credit at the initial interest rates.[1] I shall, however, in this chapter retain the assumption of fixed exchange rates. This approach enables me to measure all trade values in the currency of the home country without ambiguity and to avoid the disturbances in prices and incomes due to changing exchange rates between countries.

I assume that in all countries expenditure on consumption and investment are functions of the current level of national income. Because of the importance of the government sector in small countries, it is advisable to specify government expenditures; the assumption that in all countries government expenditures are also a function of national income is adopted.[2] Tax receipts are included as a function of national income since they obviously are. Consumption now, more realistically, depends on private disposable income. For any country, country i, consumption, investment, and government expenditures can be combined into a single domestic expenditure or absorption function, $E_i(Y_i)$. The derivative, $e_i = dE_i/dY_i$, is the marginal propensity of country i to spend on both locally produced and imported consumer, investment, and government goods and ser-

---

1. S. C. Tsaing, "The Role of Money in Trade Balance Stability: Synthesis of the Elasticity and Absorption Approaches," *American Economic Review*, LI (Dec., 1961), 924. Tsaing deplores the tradition which has neglected these factors in international trade models. I have hesitantly decided to continue this tradition in order to be able to examine the role of country size.

2. In national income models, functions for the government sector in which decisions to spend are made by elected politicians are always particularly difficult to obtain; see, for example, Wilfred Lewis, Jr.'s "The Federal Sector in National Income Models," in National Bureau of Economic Research, *Models of Income Determination* (1964). A justification for the approximation above in the case of New Zealand is offered in my article, "A Model Simulating the New Zealand Economy in the Election Year, 1963-64," *Political Science*, XVII (March, 1965), 55-72.

vices. Total imports of country i are a function of incomes, $M_i(Y_i)$. Its imports from each foreign country are also assumed to be a function of country i's income, $M_{ji}(Y_i)$. The marginal propensity to import from all countries is $m_i = dM_i/dY_i$ and the marginal propensity of the ith country to import from the jth country is $m_{ji} = dM_{ji}/dY_i$.

Let $dY_1, dY_2, \ldots, dY_n$, be the final increments of income upon any change in expenditures, for countries $1, 2, \ldots, n$, respectively. By definition, for any country, country i,

$$dY_i = dE_i + dX_i - dM_i. \qquad (1)$$

Hence,

$$\begin{aligned} dY_i &= dA_i + e_i dY_i + \sum_{j \neq i}^{n} m_{ij} dY_j - m_i dY_i, \\ &= dA_i + a_i dY_i + \sum_{j \neq i}^{n} m_{ij} dY_j. \end{aligned} \qquad (2)$$

dA_i is the increment in autonomous demand for a country's products, including its exports, and $a_i = e_i - m_i$ is its marginal propensity to spend on or to absorb its own products. Hence, for any country the equilibrium change in its income is the sum of the increments of autonomous expenditures on that country's products, increments in expenditure on its products induced by rising domestic income, and increments in its exports induced by changes in foreign incomes. From Equation (2) is obtained the following system of equations for changes in the equilibrium income of all n countries:

$$\begin{aligned} (1 - a_1) dY_1 - m_{12} dY_2 - m_{13} dY_3 - \ldots - m_{1n} dY_n &= dA_1, \\ - m_{21} dY_1 + (1 - a_2) dY_2 - m_{23} dY_3 - \ldots - m_{2n} dY_n &= dA_2, \\ \cdots \cdots \cdots \cdots \cdots \cdots \cdots \cdots \cdots \cdots \cdots \cdots \cdots \cdots \cdots \cdots \cdots & \\ - m_{n1} dY_1 - m_{n2} dY_2 - m_{n3} dY_3 - \ldots + (1 - a_n) dY_n &= dA_n. \end{aligned} \qquad (3)$$

Using matrix notation, Equation (3) may be rewritten as

$$\begin{pmatrix} (1 - a_1) & -m_{12} & \ldots & -m_{1n} \\ -m_{21} & (1 - a_2) & \ldots & -m_{2n} \\ \cdots & \cdots & \cdots & \cdots \\ -m_{n1} & -m_{n2} & \ldots & (1 - a_n) \end{pmatrix} \begin{pmatrix} dY_1 \\ dY_2 \\ \cdots \\ dY_n \end{pmatrix} = \begin{pmatrix} dA_1 \\ dA_2 \\ \cdots \\ dA_n \end{pmatrix}. \qquad (4)$$

These equations may be solved to obtain the final changes in the national income of each country, given all dA_i. An approximate solution for discrete changes in the neighborhood of the initial position can be obtained by substituting the $\triangle A_i$ values for the total differentials, dA_i, in the system of equations.

Consider the standard multiplier for the change in the income of one country, which we can call "country one," when there is a change in autonomous expenditure on the products of this country. Viz., $dA_1 \neq 0$ and all the other dA_i are zero. By Cramer's Rule, the solution for dY_1 is

$$dY_1 = \frac{dA_1 D_{11}}{D},$$

or

$$\frac{dY_1}{dA_1} = \frac{D_{11}}{D}, \tag{5}$$

where D is the determinant of the coefficient matrix in Equation (4) and D_{ij} is the co-factor of the element in the ith row and the jth column. A second set of multipliers arises when there is a change in autonomous expenditure of one foreign country, J, alone; viz., $dA_j \neq 0$ and all other dA_i are zero. The solution for country one is then

$$\frac{dY_1}{dA_j} = \frac{D_{j1}}{D}. \tag{6}$$

Expanding the determinant in the denominator of Equations (5) and (6), these equations may be rewritten in the forms[3]

$$\frac{dY_1}{dA_1} = \frac{1}{1 - a_1 - \sum_{i=2}^{n} (D_{i1}/D_{11}) m_{i1}}, \tag{7}$$

and

$$\frac{dY_1}{dA_j} = \frac{1}{(1-a_1)\frac{D_{11}}{D_{j1}} - \sum_{j \neq i}^{n} (D_{i1}/D_{j1}) m_{i1}}. \tag{8}$$

$\sum_{j \neq i}^{n} (D_{i1}/D_{j1}) m_{i1}$ are the foreign repercussions in country one. These equations show the final effect of an autonomous change in the expenditure of country one and country j, respectively, on the income of country one.

If there were only two countries in the world the expression for $\frac{dY_1}{dA_1}$ reduces to the well-known foreign trade multiplier with repercussions from the foreign country. This is

$$\frac{dY_1}{dA_1} = \frac{1}{1 - a_1 - \frac{m_1 m_2}{1 - a_2}}. \tag{9}$$

The term $\frac{m_1 m_2}{1 - a_2}$ represents the extent of the foreign repercussion on

---

3. Equation (7) is stated by Metzler, "A Multi-Region Theory," p. 345, and Chipman, "The Multi-Sector Multiplier," p. 361.

country one's exports from the increase in country two's exports and income. In this simple case, the foreign repercussion depends only on the home country's marginal propensity to import and the foreign country's marginal propensities to absorb and to import. Provided the foreign country's marginal propensity to save is positive, $1 - a_2 > m_2$, and hence $\frac{m_1 m_2}{1 - a_2} < m_1$. In spite of the favorable repercussion in this two-country model, the net effect of imports and exports in the international trade sector is to make the value of the foreign trade multiplier less than the value of the simple multiplier which would prevail if all expenditure on imports were devoted to the purchase of domestic goods.

For cases of any order, foreign repercussions (and therefore the value of the foreign trade multipliers) depend on the magnitude of the marginal propensities of all countries to absorb and import. For any country whose autonomous expenditure changes, the strength of these repercussions will be greater the greater the marginal propensities to import from this country and the greater the marginal propensities to absorb of all the countries from which it draws its own induced imports. These repercussions do not depend directly upon the share of international trade of the home country or upon "the extent to which its exports are concentrated on those countries from which it imports most," as William A. Salant contended.[4]

Yet, one may still say that the foreign repercussions of a change in domestic or foreign expenditure are likely to be negligible for small countries which are not important trading nations. This is readily seen from Equation (7) and Equation (8). If the country concerned, country one, is small, one may expect the value of all m_{1i} to be low. The smaller these m_{1i}, the smaller the foreign repercussions, given the other marginal propensities. In the limit as these m_{1i} approach zero, the value of the multiplier for any domestic change in expenditure is reduced to

$$\frac{dY_1}{dA_1} = \frac{1}{1 - a_1}. \qquad (10)$$

This implies that all imports have no multiplier effect on national income since there are no foreign repercussions on export demand for the products of this country. Of course one obtains the same multiplier if one assumes all exports to be autonomous of income in the home and foreign countries. Similarly, as all m_{1i} become smaller, the values of $\frac{dY_1}{dA_j}$ approach zero as one would expect.

---

4. "Foreign Trade Policy," p. 208.

On the other hand, as previously argued, one may expect the foreign repercussions to be significant for large countries which are important trading countries. Thus if the marginal propensities to absorb home-produced goods do not differ between large and small countries, large countries will in general have a somewhat higher value of the foreign trade multipliers than will small countries. Further, there is a reason to expect that a large country's marginal propensity to absorb its own products may be greater than that of a small country. If one assumes, in the absence of information, that the marginal propensities to spend on both home-produced and imported goods (e_i) of all countries are equal and that the marginal propensities of small countries to import are larger than those of large countries as above, then implicitly one has assumed that the marginal propensity of a small country to absorb its own products is less than that of a large country. For these reasons the formal model tends to bear out the supposition of Fritz Machlup and others that small countries will have smaller foreign repercussions and smaller values of foreign trade multipliers than large countries. However, the precise values of these foreign trade multipliers will depend on many more factors than they had envisaged.

III

More important for the purposes of this study is the total effect that autonomous changes in expenditure in a country have on its imports and balance of trade in all goods and services. Salant, Machlup, and Kindleberger all expected the increased imports which a given increase in the autonomous domestic expenditure will induce to be greater in small countries than in large countries. They also expected the foreign repercussions of the increase in autonomous expenditure in a small country on its exports to be less significant than those for a large trading country, for the increase in the imports of a small country would not stimulate world income and the repercussions on exports from the small country to any significant extent. This led Salant to believe that "a small country producing largely for exports will be able to carry through an internal expansion [only] if it takes adequate measures to protect the balance of payments." [5] But a large country, because of the small marginal propensity to import which limits the extent of the initial induced imports and because of the more favorable foreign repercussions which partly offset the small adverse movement, may be able to ignore these balance of payments aspects of a domestic expansion program. This is what Salant meant by his state-

---

5. *Ibid.*, p. 215.

ment that "large countries have greater monetary autonomy" than small countries.[6]

For the reasons elaborated in Section II small countries do tend to have lower foreign trade repercussions and lower foreign trade multipliers. It must be agreed that small countries which undertake vigorous programs of expansion are more likely to be faced with greater and probably significant deterioration in their balance of payments positions than are large countries with similar programs.

Using the theory of matrix multipliers one can state more precisely what factors will determine the final effect of a given change in autonomous expenditures in a country on the balance of trade of that country or any other country, under the assumptions of the model. These factors are of course the same factors that determine the value of the foreign trade multipliers of each country. If the change in a country's expenditure is an increase in its own domestic autonomous expenditure, for a reason such as increased government or investment expenditure, the induced increase of imports will mean an adverse movement of the country's balance of trade. This movement will be offset by the foreign repercussions. The final change after the repercussions will depend on the magnitude of the marginal propensities of each country to import goods from each foreign country and to absorb its own products. The exact change in this country's balance of trade in this case is given by the expression

$$\frac{dB_1}{dA_1} = (1 - a_1 - m_1)\frac{dY_1}{dA_1} - 1$$
$$= (1 - a_1 - m_1) \cdot \frac{1}{1 - a_1 - \sum_{i=2}^{n} (D_{i1}/D_{11}) m_{i1}} - 1. \quad (11)$$

The movement in the balance of trade in goods and services will be adverse, that is, $dB_1/dA_1 < 0$, if the marginal propensities to spend on home-produced goods plus imports $(a_i + m_i)$ are less than unity, for all n countries, as we usually assume. Further, the unfavorable movement of the balance of trade on current account must be less than the amount of the increase in autonomous expenditure.[7]

Equation (11) shows that the effect of an increase in a country's domestic expenditure on its balance of trade will be less adverse the

---

6. *Ibid.*, p. 214.
7. Metzler, "A Multi-Region Theory," p. 350, proves these theorems. The expression for the change in the balance of trade comes from the national income identity of $dB_i = dX_i - dM_i = dY_i - dE_i$. dE_i is given by the equation $dE_i = d(C_i + I_i + G_i) = dA_i + (a_i + m_i) dY_i - d_i$. d_i, the change in autonomous exports, is zero in this case.

greater its foreign trade multiplier, dY_1/dA_1. This foreign trade multiplier in turn will be greater, as we have seen, if the countries from which the home country purchases most of its imported goods have a high marginal propensity to spend and further a high marginal propensity to import goods from the home country in particular.

If the autonomous increase in country one's expenditure has its origin in an increase in this country's export receipts, the balance of payments of this country will initially improve by a commensurate amount. This initial improvement will be reduced by the combined effects of the induced increase in imports and the foreign trade repercussions. The final change in the balance of trade for this case is

$$\frac{dB_1}{dA_1} = (1 - a_1 - m_1)\frac{dY_1}{dA_1}. \qquad (12)$$

Equation (*12*) shows that the induced increase in imports due to the multiple increase in national income will exceed the initial increase in imports only if the home country's marginal propensity to spend is greater than unity.

The susceptibility of small nations to balance of payments difficulties can be illustrated by a rather special problem. Several times in the past it has been observed among such small countries as Australia, Argentina, and New Zealand that a large increase in annual export receipts has been closely followed by an increase almost as large or even larger in import payments, leaving the balance of payments little improved or in some cases in even worse condition than before the export boom. This peculiarity was debated by Kindleberger and Bloomfield in 1949. [8] I examined a similar instance in New Zealand.[9] During the twelve months of the election year ending in March, 1964, New Zealand's exports of goods and services had the largest increase ever recorded in one year—£59 million; but, within the same period, imports rose by £54 million.

Kindleberger developed a model to explain this phenomenon. It is a static model with a consumption and investment function of the same linear unlagged type as in the matrix model but without a government sector or foreign repercussions. In this case the condition that the balance of trade improve after an autonomous initial change

---

8. Charles P. Kindleberger, "The Foreign Trade Multiplier: The Propensity to Import and Balance of Payments Equilibrium," *American Economic Review,* XXXIX (March, 1949), 491–494, and *International Economics* (2nd ed.), pp. 185–186; Arthur J. Bloomfield, "Induced Investment, Overcomplete Adjustment and Chronic Dollar Shortage," *American Economic Review,* XXXIX (Sept., 1949), 970–974.

9. Lloyd, "A Model Simulating the New Zealand Economy," pp. 55–72. The conditions under which the balance of payments of nations improves in the Kindleberger and Lloyd models are derived in this study. Lloyd's model is a dynamic extension of Kindleberger's, with lagged functions and the government sector added.

in export receipts is that the marginal propensity to invest be less than the marginal propensity to save; that is, the marginal propensity to spend be less than unity. When we introduce a government sector, as in Lloyd's model,[1] the condition is still that the marginal propensity to spend including that of the government be less than unity. On the other hand, if we allow repercussions in the foreign countries, as in the matrix multiplier model, there will be a secondary increase in the exports of the home country. Yet from Equation (*12*) we have seen that the condition necessary for the final change in the balance of trade to be adverse in the model with multi-country repercussions is still that the marginal propensity of the home country to spend exceed unity. Actually, the Kindleberger and Lloyd models are simple degenerate cases of the matrix multiplier. Since all exports are regarded as autonomous in their models, all foreign repercussions vanish.

Marginal propensities to spend in excess of unity are improbable. Furthermore, when one introduces realistic expenditure lags and truncates the multiplier process, the conditions required for import payments to equal or exceed the initial increase in exports within a short period of a year or so become much more restrictive and highly unlikely.[2] However, when one also allows increases in the autonomous components of import, consumption, investment, and government expenditures as well as exports, the necessary condition is less stringent. This is so, first, because of the increase in autonomous imports itself and, second, because of the additional imports which the increase in autonomous demand for other expenditures induces. From New Zealand's experience during 1963–1964, the author surmised that the usually neglected shifts in the "autonomous" components of domestic expenditure may be even more important than the direct income effects of rising export receipts and national income in explaining the large short-run increases in import payments in these instances. Business investment expenditure may be closely related to export income via profits or the level of optimism if a boom is expected to continue. With the introduction of a government sector, the effect of an initial increase in export earnings on total spending depends to a considerable degree on the extent to which rising taxation receipts and other factors induce the government sector to increase its own expenditures on goods and services and on transfer payments. Part of these changes in business and government expenditure must be regarded as shifts of the expenditure function. These shifts of "autonomous" expendi-

---

1. *Ibid.*
2. For the model without foreign repercussions, truncated multipliers for any number of income periods are easily derived (*ibid.*, Appendix).

tures are distinguished from the direct effects of rising incomes via the marginal propensities, but they are indirectly related to the rising export receipts via rising personal and business optimism and the reactions of politicians to these changes through such actions as the relaxation of direct import licensing[3] or other controls.

Such shifts of the domestic expenditure function during an export boom are quite possible in small countries where the export and government sectors are relatively large. In the selected fifteen small developed countries, government expenditure on current goods and services alone ranged from 13 per cent to 21 per cent of total spending in 1964.[4] The existence of shifts in the domestic expenditure function eliminates the need for quite unrealistically high values of the marginal propensity to spend in order to explain the phenomenon of an export boom which leads to an adverse movement of the balance of payments. (A dependence of taxation receipts on export incomes in developing countries and the destabilizing consequences of this dependence have been observed by others.)[5]

As noted at the outset, this model is greatly simplified in that it does not explicitly treat aggregate supply, the money sector, or real-balance effects of changes in the price level. Changes in overseas assets of residents and the banking system, for example, may have important repercussions on credit and spending in small countries that could intensify the export boom and its effects on the imports and the balance of trade if unchecked. Nevertheless the foreign trade multipliers play a central part in the short-run behavior of an economy.

The importance of the tendency of small countries to have low repercussions and balance of payments difficulties is obvious. Essentially, this tendency means that the common conflict between the dual objectives of a satisfactory rate of economic growth and balance of payments stability may be more difficult to achieve jointly in some small developed countries than in large developed countries. The growth ambitions of small nations, which (as noted in Chapter III) are dependent on imports for more than 50 per cent of their fixed capital goods and the development of their industrial sectors, may be constrained by a "trade gap."

---

3. This factor appeared to be particularly important in the New Zealand instance. New Zealand has maintained import licensing of varying severity since 1938.
4. United Nations, *Yearbook of National Accounts Statistics,* 1965.
5. H. H. Hinrichs, "Determinants of Government Revenue Shares among Less Developed Countries," *Economic Journal,* LXXV (Sept., 1965), 546–556; Wallich, "Underdeveloped Countries." Reynolds, "Domestic Consequences," offers a similar model of the underdeveloped Chilean economy.

Appendix to Chapter IV

Here we explore relationships between the foreign trade multiplier, dY_1/dA_1, and size of country under certain restrictive assumptions. We begin with a brief look at the three-country model.

When $n = 3$, Equation (7) reduces to

$$\frac{dY_1}{dA_1} = \frac{1}{1 - a_1 - \left\{\dfrac{+ m_{21}[m_{12}(1-a_3) + m_{13}m_{12}] + m_{31}[m_{23}m_{12} + m_{13}(1-a_2)]}{(1-a_2)(1-a_3) - m_{32}m_{23}}\right\}} \qquad (13)$$

The terms m_{21} and m_{31} in the denominator of Equation (13) give the induced imports of country one that arise because of the change in domestic expenditure. The other terms in the bracketed expressions represent the foreign repercussions per unit of induced imports. The expression for these repercussions is more complex in the three-country case than in the two-country case because it must take into account the repercussions between the home country and two foreign countries and also the repercussions between the two foreign countries themselves.

This formula may be greatly simplified when we make assumptions of symmetry in the pattern of international trade such as were first used by Fritz Machlup. Let all countries be "of approximately equal importance in the trade relations with one another";[1] viz., let all the marginal propensities of each country to import from each of the other foreign countries be identical. Then $m_{ij} = m_{ji}$ for all i and j. Further, assume that the marginal propensities of all countries to absorb are equal.

Equation (13) is now given by

$$\frac{dY_1}{dA_1} = \frac{1}{1 - a_1 - \dfrac{2(m_{ij})^2}{1 - a_j - m_{ij}}}. \qquad (14)$$

---

1. Machlup, *International Trade*, p. 92.

Appendix to Chapter IV

If the term m_j represents the total marginal propensity to import of the jth country, then $m_j = 2m_{ij}$, or $m_{ij} = m_j/2$. Equation *(14)* may then be written as

$$\frac{dY_1}{dA_1} = \frac{1}{1 - a_1 - m_1 \left[\dfrac{m_j}{2(1 - a_j - \dfrac{m_j}{2})} \right]} \qquad (15)$$

where j may be either country two or country three.

A comparison of Equation *(15)* with Equation *(9)* shows that the effect of the introduction of the third country, when it is assumed to be similar to the initial two countries, is to reduce the value of the foreign repercussions. Therefore the value of the foreign trade multiplier itself is reduced. More exactly, the value of the foreign repercussion is approximately halved, since the marginal propensity of each country to import goods from the other two countries is assumed to be equal for all countries. Therefore, only one-half of the change in the demand of country two and country three for imported products will be for the goods of country one, which is here assumed to have had the initial autonomous change in expenditure.

The basic characteristics of the symmetric many-country model are already exhibited by the three-country model above. Machlup discussed an arithmetic example in which there are eleven countries "of approximately equal importance in the trade relations among one another." He illustrated arithmetically the proposition that "the larger the number of [identical] foreign countries, the smaller will be the foreign repercussion upon [the home] country A." [2] He did not, however, prove this proposition. Machlup also ventured the view that "the larger the world outside of A, regarded as one super-country made up of all foreign countries, the smaller would be the marginal propensity to import in this super-country and, therefore, the smaller the foreign repercussion upon country A." [3] His lack of a general solution to the n-country case as provided by Metzler and Chipman prevented him from proving these propositions.

---

2. *Ibid.*, p. 93, n. 1. Machlup considers only the special case in which $dE_1 = -dE_2$. This case is exactly analogous to the celebrated Transfer Problem because of a reparations payment in which as one possibility we may assume that the income of the paying country falls and that of the receiving country rises by an amount identical to the reparations payment. This case is of course simply the combination of the two cases discussed in the text in which, on the one hand, the expenditure change originates in the home country and, on the other, originates in one foreign country. It will also occur when there is a shift of absorption expenditure from foreign sources to domestic sources in the home country.

3. *Ibid.*

We can extend rigorously Machlup's symmetry propositions to n countries using the matrix multiplier. The matrix of coefficients in which all diagonal elements equal $(1-a)$ and all the off-diagonal elements are equal for all m_{ij}, suppressing subscripts, has the determinant

$$D = \begin{vmatrix} 1-a & -m & \ldots & -m \\ -m & 1-a & \ldots & -m \\ \vdots & & & \vdots \\ -m & -m & \ldots & 1-a \end{vmatrix}.$$

Adding the first $(n-1)$ rows to the last row

$$D = \begin{vmatrix} 1-a & -m & \ldots & -m \\ -m & 1-a & \ldots & -m \\ \vdots & & & \vdots \\ (1-a)-(n-1)m & (1-a)-(n-1)m & \ldots & (1-a)-(n-1)m \end{vmatrix}.$$

Factoring $[(1-a)-(n-1)m]$ and adding to each of the first $(n-1)$ rows m times the last row

$$D = [(1-a)-(n-1)m] \begin{vmatrix} (1-a)+m & 0 & \ldots & 0 & 0 \\ 0 & (1-a)+m & \ldots & 0 & 0 \\ \vdots & \vdots & \ldots & (1-a)+m & 0 \\ 1 & 1 & \ldots & 1 & 1 \end{vmatrix}$$

$$= (1-a+m)^{n-1}[(1-a)-(n-1)m].\ ^{4}$$
(16)

Hence

$$\frac{dY_1}{dA_1} = \frac{D_{11}}{D} = \frac{[(1-a)+m]^{n-2}[(1-a)-(n-2)m]}{[(1-a)+m]^{n-1}[(1-a)-(n-1)m]}$$

$$= \frac{1}{1-a-\dfrac{(n-1)m^2}{1-a-(n-2)m}} \quad (17)$$

Where $n = 3$, Equation (17) agrees with Equation (14).

As in the three-country case, let m_j represent the total marginal propensity to import of country j. Since the marginal propensity of each country to import goods from each other country is assumed to be equal, viz.,

$$m_j = \sum_{j \neq i}^{n} m_{ij} = (n-1)m_{ij},$$

or

$$m_{ij} = \frac{m_j}{(n-1)}.$$

---

4. I owe this simple proof to John Kinney of the Mathematics Department at Michigan State University.

Appendix to Chapter IV

Equation (17) becomes

$$\frac{dY_1}{dA_1} = \frac{I'}{1 - a_1 - m_1 \cdot \dfrac{m_j}{n-1}\left[\dfrac{1}{1 - a_j - (n-2)\dfrac{m_i}{n-1}}\right]} \qquad (18)$$

The term $\left[\dfrac{1}{1 - a_j - (n-2)\dfrac{m_i}{n-1}}\right]$ in the denominator represents the multiplier effect on the national income of each of the foreign countries whose exports and national income increase because of the initial increase in the imports of country one. The portion of each country's increased imports purchased from country one is represented by $m_j/n - 1$. For a given value of m_j, the larger the number of (symmetric) foreign countries, the smaller the value of $m_j/n - 1$ and therefore the smaller the value of the foreign repercussion and, *ceteris paribus*, the smaller the value of the foreign trade multiplier.

The assumption that all countries "are of approximately equal importance in the relations among one another" implies that the absolute value of foreign trade is approximately equal in all n countries and further that the trade of all countries is equally distributed among all $n - 1$ foreign countries. Moreover, these assumptions imply that all countries are of approximately equal size in terms of national income, if one makes the further assumption that countries of equal trading importance are of approximately equal size in terms of national income. Thus the model appears to rule out the very factor in which we are chiefly interested: the significance of the size of nations.

Fortunately one may introduce the factor of varying national size by the device of presuming that certain of these "identical" countries amalgamate.[5] Those units which were previously sovereign nations are now regarded as integral parts of larger countries. Assume that the pattern of exchange among the units as initially constituted is unaltered. Hence, the absolute value of the foreign trade of each nation increases—though not proportionately and only up to a point—with the size of the country, that is, with the number of units that now comprise the nation. This process of hypothetical amalgamation also implies that each nation distributes its export and import trade among

---

5. This same device has been used in different contexts by Jan Tinbergen, "Customs Unions: Influence of Their Size on Their Effect," *Zeitschrift für die gesamte Staatswissenschaft*, Ed. 113, No. 2 (1957), pp. 404–414, and also by Guy Orcutt, "Exchange Rate Adjustment and Relative Size of the Depreciating Bloc," *Review of Economics and Statistics*, XXXVII (Feb., 1955), chap. v.

the foreign nations in proportion to the size of these newly formed nations. This case is not altogether unrealistic. As a first approximation, small countries tend to conduct the bulk of their export and import trade with one of the largest trading nations, and to the large trading nations this volume of trade constitutes only a small share of their total export and import trade. This is, in essence, the significance of the above assumption.

Consider the case of a relatively small country so formed. If an autonomous change in expenditure occurs in this home country or in any of the other countries, large or small, the extent of the foreign repercussions on the exports of this small country will be exactly the same as in the case of n countries of identical size. However, in this case Equation (18) has to be slightly amended. The magnitude of the foreign repercussion for the small country will be in direct proportion to its share of world income, rather than in direct proportion to the number of countries in the rest of the world. That is, it depends on its size, in terms of national income, vis-à-vis the rest of the world's income.

A similar theorem can be proven for the multipliers dY_1/dA_j. Hence, the simple correspondence between increases in the size of the country in relation to the size of the rest of the world and increases in the value of the foreign repercussions and foreign trade multipliers rests on the assumption of symmetry in all world trade. If one does not make this assumption, then the various foreign trade multipliers are given by the more complex formulas of Equations (7) and (8), or some combination of them.

CHAPTER V

Devaluation by a Small Nation

I

Despite repeated criticism from several quarters, the gold-exchange standard established by the Bretton Woods Agreement of 1944 remains essentially unchanged. Under this standard, countries are supposed to adjust the pegged values of their exchange rates in the event of a "fundamental disequilibrium." Past arguments have led many to expect that such fundamental disturbances to the balance of payments occur more frequently in small countries. Coppock's statistics cited in Chapter III indicated that only three of thirteen small countries for which statistics were available had more than the average amount of instability in their annual export receipts. All the small countries have, however, at times in the postwar period gone through balance of payments disturbances. Yet the small nations of this study seem to have resisted devaluation or appreciation of their currencies as vigorously as most nations in this period. Since the 1949 adjustment of exchange rates which was precipitated by the devaluation of pound sterling, only Austria (1953), Israel (1952 and 1962), Finland (1957), and Venezuela (1964) have devalued their currencies. Israel is the only one of these countries to have devalued twice.[1] The Dutch guilder was appreciated by 3 per cent in 1961. Nevertheless, revaluation of exchange rates remains an ever-present alternative to other policies. In this chapter I shall consider whether devaluation by a small nation is likely to correct an adverse balance of payments disturbance. Several a priori arguments have been made concerning small countries which

---

1. I am ignoring small changes in the multiple exchange rates of some of these countries. In the first ten years of its existence Israel maintained multiple rates. Finland abolished her multiple exchange rates at the time of the 1957 devaluation. In May, 1953, Austria established a single exchange rate at 26 schillings per U.S. dollar. This meant a de facto devaluation for commodity trade which had previously been traded at an average rate of 21.36 schillings per U.S. dollar. The official exchange rate of Venezuelan bolivar has remained unchanged since 1947, but Venezuela maintains multiple exchange rates and the selling rate which is taken as the rate was devalued by 34 percent in 1964 (International Monetary Fund, *International Financial Statistics* [July, 1966], p. 25).

devalue. One in particular, concerning the foreign elasticity of demand for exports of small nations, has been advanced on many occasions to suggest that a devaluation is likely to be effective in a small country. After evaluating and restating these arguments we shall be able to make certain observations.

The traditional analysis of the effect of devaluation (or appreciation) of a country's exchange rate on the devaluing country's balance of trade is in terms of the "four elasticities" of export and import trade in a two-country, two-good model.[2] Earlier writers treated these elasticities as partial elasticities, holding constant or ignoring changes in incomes and the prices of non-traded goods. Subsequently many objections have been made against the appropriateness of using such partial elasticities to predict the final change in the balance of payments. The implied assumption that in each country the import demand and export supply curves remain unchanged after devaluation, in terms of the currency of the respective home country, is obviously quite unrealistic. Changes in the relative price structure and in incomes that will occur as a result of the devaluation itself will cause all schedules to shift. The *ceteris paribus* assumptions used in many industry and sector studies are invalid when the sector—in this case the international sector—is large in relation to national product and the price (exchange rate) which is changed affects all transactions in this sector.

It is now realized that in the formulas which express the *final* effect of devaluation on the balance of trade in terms of the four elasticities, the elasticities should be interpreted not as partial elasticities but as "total elasticities" which reflect all the direct and indirect changes of relative prices and incomes resulting from devaluation. However, these relationships in terms of total elasticities are purely definitional; they reveal nothing of the underlying mechanism. Nor do they permit any predictions of the effects of a devaluation, unless all the monetary and fiscal factors are fully specified in a model combining simultaneously income and price effects. Some very elegant models which do combine income and price effects have been constructed by several authors (Tsiang, Meade, Kemp, *et al.*).[3] Not only are these models

---

2. This tradition stems from celebrated articles by C. F. Bickerdike and Joan Robinson. For a lucid account of the development of the "elasticities" approach to devaluation, see Lloyd Metzler, "The Theory of International Trade," in *Survey of Contemporary Economics,* ed. H. S. Ellis (Homewood, Ill., 1948), I, 228–232.

3. Some of the alternative models are discussed most fully by S. C. Tsiang, "The Role of Money in Trade Balance Stability," pp. 912–936, and Murray Kemp, *The Pure Theory of International Trade* (Englewood Cliffs, N.J., 1964), chap. xvi.

complex but there are also unlimited ways of constructing such general equilibrium models.

Another possibility is to use the "four elasticities" formulas for the prediction of "primary" or initial effect of devaluation on the balance of trade, temporarily ignoring "secondary" effects on income and prices. This initial effect is expressed in terms of the partial elasticities of demand and supply for imports and exports. Secondary effects on income and also prices are then considered as reversing the primary price effect. This procedure is not wholly satisfactory since it ignores all the interaction that will occur between income and cross-price effects. It does not, however, seem possible to introduce size into more comprehensive models in a systematic way. Moreover, we still have to consider the arguments concerning the possible effects of country size on the primary effects in particular, and almost all writers who have considered country size in relation to devaluation have followed this dichotomy of treating primary and secondary effects separately. Below I shall therefore consider in turn the possible relationships between country size and the primary and secondary effects of a devaluation.

II

Let one country, which we shall call the home country, devalue its currency by a discrete amount in terms of the currency of the foreign country. The foreign country can be interpreted as the "rest of the world." The "primary" or initial change in the trade balance of the home country after devaluation can be stated in terms of the four partial price elasticities for the (homogeneous) export good and import good, holding the prices of non-traded goods and incomes constant. The four price elasticities are the elasticity of the home country's demand for imports (ϵ_h), the elasticity of the home country's supply of its export good (η_h), the elasticity of the rest of the world's demand for the exports of the home country (ϵ_f), and the elasticity of the rest of the world's supply of the import good to the home country (η_f). Elasticities of demand are defined as positive when the demand curve is negatively sloped. Hence, all trade elasticities will normally be positive.

The change in the home country's balance of trade, expressed in units of the foreign currency, is given approximately (ignoring second and higher order terms) by the expression

$$E_f = \frac{\Delta B_f}{X_f} / k \approx \frac{\eta_h(\epsilon_f - 1)}{\eta_h + \epsilon_f(1-k)} + \frac{M_f}{X_f} \cdot \frac{\epsilon_h(\eta_f + 1)}{\eta_f(1-k) + \epsilon_h} \qquad (1)$$

where k is the proportion by which the foreign price of the devalued currency falls. X_f and M_f are the pre-devaluation values of export receipts and import payments, measured in foreign currency. All elasticities are expressed in terms of the initial prices and quantities demanded and supplied in the countries to which the schedules relate. The term E_f is referred to as the elasticity of the balance of payments (in foreign currency) with respect to a change in the exchange rate. The effect of devaluation on capital account transactions and the possibility of speculations and of second country retaliation are ignored.[4] In practice these may be important considerations though small countries whose currencies are not held as reserve currencies and whose capital markets are less developed are usually less concerned with these factors than large countries.

When the balance of trade is expressed in terms of the currency of the home country, its expression differs from that given above in terms of the foreign currency (except in the special and uninteresting case in which trade is balanced before devaluation).[5] In considering the effect of devaluation on the balance of payments itself, the balance expressed in terms of the foreign currency is the relevant balance. However, when estimating the "secondary" effect of a devaluation through changes in domestic incomes or the price level, the relevant balance is that expressed in domestic currency.

The relationship between the size of a nation and the magnitude of the primary effect of a currency devaluation hinges on whether this primary effect is increased or decreased by higher elasticities of demand and supply at home and in the rest of the world. It can be readily shown that the change in the balance of trade (in terms of either the foreign or the domestic currency) will be more favorable, the greater the elasticity of home demand ϵ_h, the greater the elasticity of foreign demand ϵ_f, the greater the elasticity of home supply η_h (provided the elasticity of foreign demand is itself greater than unity), and the greater the elasticity of foreign supply η_f (provided the elasticity of home demand is greater than unity).[6] No direct

---

4. I shall be concerned solely with devaluation as a means of improving the balance of trade. I shall not discuss devaluation as a method of relaxing import controls nor comment explicitly on the effects of devaluation on the terms of trade, national income, or other variables.

5. The formulas for the change in the balance, in terms of both the home and the foreign currency, have been derived many times, and the derivations are therefore omitted here. Sydney Alexander, "The Effects of Devaluation: A Simplified Synthesis of Elasticities and Absorption Approaches," *American Economic Review*, XLIX (March, 1959), Appendix, derives the same expression as in Equation (*1*) above and the analogous expression for the balance in the home currency. The use of the discrete adjustments seems preferable to the more common use of infinitely small adjustments in this context. The expressions in terms of derivatives can be obtained simply by taking the limits of the discrete formulas if one wishes.

6. These propositions can be verified by differentiating partially E_f of Equation

Devaluation by a Small Nation

estimates of these trade elasticities are available for the small countries. However, an important hypothesis relating the size of country to the elasticity of foreign demand for its exports has been made and will be examined now.

It has been frequently asserted, on analogy with the theory of perfect competition, that the foreign demand for the products of a small country will normally be highly elastic.[7] Under competitive conditions, the demand curve for the product of a single firm as a price-taker among many other firms is almost perfectly elastic, whereas the demand curve for the product of the industry as a whole is less elastic and may be quite inelastic. By analogy, the price elasticity of foreign demand for exports tends to be more elastic, it is claimed, for small countries (or more precisely for countries whose exports constitute a small part of the world's markets), since the possibility of substituting a small country's sales vis-à-vis those of another producing country's are enhanced. This is the so-called importance-of-being-unimportant assumption. (No such claim for high elasticities has been made for developing countries because of the assumed inelasticity of demand for the primary products they export in the main and the generally large share of export markets which they occupy in these commodities.)[8]

The assumed small export share of small countries and the associated elastic foreign demand for the exports of small countries have been commonly held to make the primary effect of devaluation by a small country very favorable. This is the reason many authors claim that a

---

(1), and the analogous expression in terms of home currency, with respect to the four elasticities, ϵ_h, ϵ_f, η_h, and η_f, respectively.

The propositions only apply strictly under two conditions: first, all trade elasticities, as defined, are positive; and second, all elasticities are independent of each other. In fact, all four elasticities may be interdependent because of numerous relationships of substitution and complementarity in both production and consumption. For example, when exports have an import content, η_h and ϵ_h are interrelated. Further examples of interrelation between all four elasticities are given by T. Balogh and P. P. Streeten, "The Inappropriateness of Simple 'Elasticity' Concepts in the Analysis of International Trade," *Bulletin of Oxford University Institute of Statistics*, XIII (March, 1957), 67–69.

7. As a sample, see Metzler, "Theory of International Trade," p. 230; Orcutt, "Exchange Rate Adjustment," p. 1; F. B. Horner, "Elasticity of Demand for the Exports of a Single Country," *Review of Economics and Statistics*, XXXIV (Nov., 1952), 326; Randall Hinshaw, "Further Comment," *Quarterly Journal of Economics*, LII (Nov., 1958), 625.

8. One factor that will qualify the relationship between market shares and elasticity of demand is the existence of non-homogeneity and differentiation of products. Primary products are more homogeneous than most manufactures and this will tend to raise the elasticity of demand for exports of primary products vis-à-vis manufactures. However, the existence of close substitutes, the nature of demand, tariffs, and transport costs, may lower the elasticity of demand for primary products more than they do the elasticity of demand for most manufactures.

devaluation by a small country is likely to be effective.[9] Of course, the effectiveness or effect of a devaluation on the balance of payments depends, above all, on the proportion by which the currency is devalued. Very few of those who have claimed that devaluation in a small country will be effective have indicated even the approximate proportion of devaluation they have in mind. The main advantage to a small country of high trade elasticities is that, other things being equal, it could eliminate a balance of payments disequilibrium by devaluing by a smaller proportion than would otherwise be required.

The relationship between elasticity of demand and market shares has also been derived directly by several of the writers who argue that a small country has an elastic foreign demand for its export good.[1] The quantity imported by the rest of the world is equal to the difference between the rest of the world's production and absorption of the homogeneous good. These writers assume that all quantities of the export good demanded and supplied in the rest of the world are functions of own price alone, and that world price is everywhere identical at ruling exchange rates. The expression for the foreign elasticity of demand for imports is obtained simply by differentiating the demand and supply functions of this good in this equation, dividing by the original price, and substituting the appropriate elasticity terms. The resulting expression is

$$\epsilon_f = \frac{D_{fx}}{x} \cdot \epsilon_{fx} + \frac{S_{fx}}{x} \cdot \eta_{fx}. \quad (2)$$

D_{fx}, S_{fx}, x, are the quantities of the good demanded, supplied, and imported by the rest of the world at the original price. The elasticity of the rest of the world's demand for the exports of the home country is then some multiple of the component elasticities of total demand (ϵ_{fx}) and supply (η_{fx}) for the good in the rest of the world.

It is clear from Equation (2) that $\epsilon_f > \epsilon_{fx}$ except in the limiting case where there is no production of the good in the rest of the world before the price change. It should be noted that, by assumption, this expression rules out all income, cross-price effects, product differentiation, tariffs, and transport costs that in practice also affect the elasticity of demand for a product. From Equation (2) it also follows that foreign demand for the home country's exports will be more elastic

---

9. For example, Orcutt, "Exchange Rate Adjustment," p. 1; Metzler, "Theory of International Trade," p. 230; Marcus Fleming, "Exchange Depreciation, Financial Policy, and the Domestic Price Level," International Monetary Fund, *Staff Papers*, VII (April, 1958), 301.

1. Orcutt, "Exchange Rate Adjustment," Appendix; Horner, "Elasticity of Demand," p. 327; Fleming, "Exchange Depreciation," Appendix.

the greater the foreign elasticity of demand for the export good, the greater the rest of the world's elasticity of supply of this good, and the larger the proportion of the rest of the world's absorption of this good that is produced in the rest of the world itself, viz., the smaller the devaluing country's share of the rest of the world's markets. In the extreme case in which the market share of the devaluing country is very small indeed, the elasticity of foreign demand for its exports approaches infinity, and the country is an international export price-taker.[2]

The proposition concerning the elasticity of foreign demand for a country's exports is sometimes expressed in the form that this elasticity is a function of the number of countries producing the export good in the markets of the rest of the world.[3] Formally one may derive the expression for the elasticity of the rest of the world's demand for the home country's exports as the sum of the weighted averages of the elasticities of demand for the export good and the elasticities of supply of the good in each of the countries in the rest of the world. The weights are the quantities absorbed and produced respectively in each country. (The same procedure can be applied to the other three trade elasticities.)[4] Obviously if more than one country devalues at the same time, the elasticity of foreign demand facing these countries as a group would be considerably less than the elasticity of demand for the product of a small country devaluing its currency alone.

Up to now the assumption that there is only one homogeneous export good and one homogeneous import good has been followed. In reality exports and imports are aggregates of very many commodities. It is possible conceptually to construct elasticities of demand and supply for traded goods as weighted averages of the estimates for the individual export and import products. There are in practice many obstacles to the empirical calculation of average elasticities because of complementarity and substitutability among traded goods, the selection of weights, and other factors. Furthermore, the omission of potential export and import goods from the calculation of the weighted elasticities of demand and supply in any country will understate the

---

2. Note that if the prices of imports (in foreign currency) are also fixed as a price-taker, which is more plausible, then the terms of trade of such countries are also fixed and unaffected by devaluation.

3. For example, Fritz Machlup, "The Theory of Foreign Exchanges," in *Readings in the Theory of International Trade*, p. 118, and Elliott Zupnick and Robert M. Stern, "Devaluation in a Three-Country World," *Economia Internazionale*, XVII (Nov., 1964).

4. Orcutt, "Exchange Rate Adjustment," Appendix; Zupnick and Stern, "Devaluation in a Three-Country World."

relevant average elasticities. It is probable that in small countries such shifts of production among industries will be slow because of the narrow range of goods produced and the associated limited number of potential trade goods. Consequently, the understatement of their elasticities resulting from this factor may not be great.

Michael Michaely has shown that the weighted average elasticity of foreign demand for a country's actual export products, defined as the proportionate change in the average foreign price of these exports for a given equal proportionate change in their quantities, is, under certain simplifications, approximately equal to $\epsilon_f^* \frac{1}{W_{jx}}$.[5] The commodity-weighted share of a country in world export trade (W_{jx}) was defined and employed in Chapter III; ϵ_f^* is the elasticity of foreign demand for the country's "typical" exports. Obviously, the lower a country's commodity-weighted share of trade, the higher its foreign elasticity of demand. Michaely's weighted average foreign elasticities of demand ignore all cross-price substitutions, all potential trade goods, as does the formula for ϵ_f in Equation (2), and the possibility of substitution on devaluation of the exporting country's goods for the domestic production in the foreign markets. Yet the results are still very significant. Only two (Austria and Norway) of ten small countries for which his statistics are available had commodity-weighted shares of less than 10 per cent of world exports.[6] The fact that exports of each small country comprise less than 4 per cent of total world export trade is offset by the tendency for their exports to be concentrated on only a few of all the products traded internationally. The net result is that the small countries do *not* in general have small commodity-weighted shares of world export trade as previous writers on devaluation have claimed. This was confirmed by statistics of individual export commodities. Some small countries—especially the primary products exporters, Finland, Sweden, Australia, and New Zealand—are the largest suppliers of their main export products in world markets. In several cases they supply more than 50 per cent of total world export trade.[7] These statistics refute conclusively the very common contention that the foreign elasticity of demand for the exports of a small country is necessarily high enough to insure that a small devaluation by a small country will be effective in improving the balance of payments.

III

The slightly different question of the effectiveness of devaluation (by

---
5. Michaely, *Concentration in International Trade*, chap. iv.
6. *Ibid.*, pp. 31-32.
7. See chap. iii, sec. i, above.

a given proportion) in a small nation vis-à-vis its effectiveness in a large nation has been considered by only a few authors.[8] Orcutt cautions against extending the idea that devaluation may be effective in a small nation because of the relatively high elasticity of foreign demand for its exports (which he accepts) to the idea that devaluation by a large country or bloc of countries is less effective. The probable values of the other trade elasticities in both large and small countries must also be considered.

Expressions for the three other elasticities ϵ_h, η_h, and η_f may be derived from the underlying demand and supply schedules for the export and import goods in the home country and the rest of the world in the same way as the expression in Equation (2) for ϵ_f was derived. All three elasticities have the same form as that for the elasticity of the rest of the world's demand for the home country's exports in Equation (2).[9] These elasticities are weighted averages of the elasticities of demand and supply of the export or import good, in which the weights are respectively the ratios of the original quantities demanded and supplied in the relevant country to the quantities of this good traded internationally.

All three elasticities will be greater the greater the relevant elasticities of total demand and supply for the export or import good in the home country or the rest of the world. More important for the question of country size and its relationship to the four trade elasticities, the following propositions can be derived. The elasticity of the home country's demand for imports (ϵ_h) will be greater the greater the proportion of the home country's total absorption of the import good that is produced at home; the elasticity of home supply of exports (η_h) will be greater the greater the proportion of the home country's total production of this good which is absorbed domestically; the elasticity of the rest of the world's supply of the home country's imports (η_f) will be greater the greater the proportion of the rest of the world's total production of this good which is absorbed in the rest of the world itself.

From this division of each of the four elasticities into its two constituent elasticities, further insights into the determinants of the four

---

8. Orcutt, "Exchange Rate Adjustment"; Fleming, "Exchange Depreciation," pp. 296–301; Michaely, *Concentration in International Trade,* chap. iv.

9. All these elasticities are derived and specified by several authors: Orcutt, "Exchange Rate Adjustment," Appendix; E. V. Morgan, "The Theory of Flexible Exchange Rates," *American Economic Review,* XLV (June, 1955), 280; Fleming, "Exchange Depreciation," pp. 293–298; *et al.*

The first algebraic statement of these export supply and import demand equations in terms of the component elasticities appears to be that by Theodore Yntema, *A Mathematical Reformulation of the General Theory of International Trade* (Chicago, 1932), chap. iv.

elasticities and the role of country size are possible. As Marcus Fleming stated it, "since the outside world (non-A) will normally be much larger economically than A, the ratio of absorption to output will normally be nearer to unity in non-A than in A. Mainly for this reason, the foreign trade elasticities will normally be greater in non-A than in A." [1] That is, in all countries, the elasticities ϵ_f and η_f will tend to be greater than ϵ_h and η_h. This tendency will apply to both large and small countries vis-à-vis the rest of the world, but it will apply with particular force to small countries having a highly specialized production and trade. In these countries the nature of their specialization for international trade will mean that only a small part of the total production of the goods exported will be absorbed at home and only a small part of the total absorption of any of the goods they import will be produced domestically. As the "eight elasticities" model illustrated, this implies a lower domestic elasticity of demand for imports and elasticity of supply of exports, *ceteris paribus*, than in large countries. On this basis Fleming made the generalization that "large countries tend to have higher foreign trade elasticities at home [ϵ_h and η_h] and tend to encounter lower foreign trade elasticities abroad [ϵ_f and η_f] than do small countries of the same type." [2]

Another reason for expecting lower elasticities of demand for imports in small countries appears when we recognize the preponderance of imports of "essential" raw materials and fixed capital goods in small countries and the lack of domestic substitutes.[3] Further, the more limited range of production in smaller countries may mean they generally have fewer potential trade goods which can be exported after a devaluation than do large countries. This factor would make for lower elasticities of supply of exports than in larger countries, other things being equal.

Since the primary effects of devaluation depend on all four trade elasticities, one cannot say on a priori grounds that devaluation of the currency of a small country is likely to be more effective than that of a large country. Orcutt demonstrated this in his statement of the "eight elasticities" model, which contains a world of M countries so defined that their initial consumption of each of the two goods, one import and one export good, are equal. Orcutt adopts the device of hypothetically varying the number of units that comprise the two blocs,

---

1. Fleming, "Exchange Depreciation," p. 296.
2. *Ibid.*, p. 300. The elasticities symbols have been changed in the quotation to conform to those used in this chapter.
3. See chap. iii, above. These same factors will apply in some developing countries; Carlos Diaz Alejandro, *Exchange Rate Devaluation in a Semi-Industrialized Country* (Cambridge, Mass., 1965), p. 50.

Devaluation by a Small Nation

the devaluing bloc which consists of the first m of the M units and the rest of the world or the $M - m$ units. This varies the size of the devaluing bloc vis-à-vis the rest of the world. He uses the elasticity of the balance of payments with respect to a change in the exchange rate as the measure of the effectiveness of a devaluation.[4]

As the size of the devaluing country is varied, the ratio of the quantity of the import good produced to the total quantity consumed, which he calls the "measure of self-sufficiency," also varies. For assumed realistic values of the self-sufficiency ratios for various sizes of the two blocs and varying values of the eight elasticities, Orcutt concludes that "neglecting secondary repercussions, exchange rate adjustments between such large blocs as the dollar area and the rest of the world would in general be more effective in bringing about balance of payments adjustments than would exchange rate adjustments between a small country and the rest of the world." [5]

Fleming's more comprehensive model yields the opposite conclusion. On the basis of what Fleming considers to be probable numerical values of the four elasticities, he finds that the improvement in the small country is considerably greater than that in the large country of the same type. This conclusion applies to the case of a small primary-producing vis-à-vis a large primary-producing country and to the case of a small industrial vis-à-vis a large industrial country. These results are partly the outcome of high values of both the elasticities of foreign demand for exports and foreign supply of imports for a small country which Fleming chooses.[6] In general, we can only say that whether the primary effect of a given devaluation in a small country is likely to be more favorable than in a large country will depend on the precise values assumed for all the elasticity parameters.

IV

Now consider the secondary aspects of devaluation. I stated earlier that the final effect of a devaluation may be crudely taken as the sum

---

4. To be exact, he uses the measure $\dfrac{dB}{X+M} \div k$.
5. Orcutt, "Exchange Rate Adjustment," p. 8.
6. Fleming, "Exchange Depreciation," pp. 301–303, and Table 2. Fleming expresses the change in the balance of trade as a proportion of total national output rather than exports plus imports as in Orcutt's expression. This approach tends to exaggerate the percentage improvement in the balance of trade for small countries since the foreign trade sector is larger in relation to the national output. However, this accounts for only a part of the considerable difference in the effectiveness of devaluation in small and large countries in Fleming's examples.

Both Orcutt and Fleming ignore the important consideration that the danger of other countries' devaluing their currencies in defense (as after the British devaluation in 1949) is much greater for large countries. Such an occurrence, of course, increases the size of the devaluing bloc vis-à-vis the rest of the world.

of primary and secondary effects. In contrast to the optimism concerning the primary effect of a devaluation in a small country, we shall see that several reasons have been put forward to suggest that the secondary effects on incomes and prices may be particularly adverse in small countries. I shall presume below that the trade elasticities are at least sufficiently high to insure that the balance of trade in goods and services is improved by the primary effect of a devaluation.

The absorption approach to devaluation stresses that any initial change in the balance of trade, in terms of the home currency, itself implies either an increase in the current value of national income or a decrease in national absorption or possibly an increase in national income which is greater than an increase in the value of national absorption. (Note that with a trade deficit before devaluation, the change in the balance of payments measured in terms of the *home* currency upon devaluation must always be less than the change in terms of foreign currency, when converted at the post-devaluation rate of exchange. Indeed, if the improvement in the foreign balance is less than the devaluation percentage decrease in the number of units of foreign currency per unit of domestic currency, the balance in the home currency will "deteriorate.") These changes in national income and domestic expenditure which accompany the primary improvement in the trade balance, unless counteracted, are the multiplicand initiating a further expansion of national income. The multiplier in turn induces a whole chain of price and income effects that will have a "secondary" impact on the balance of payments.

The multiple increase in national income will directly increase imports via the marginal propensity to import and offset the primary effect of a devaluation. In the previous chapter it was reasoned that the multiplier for a given change in domestic autonomous expenditure, such as that due to the primary effect of a devaluation on the trade balance in the home currency, would be lower in a small country than in a large country. This is so because of the higher marginal propensity to import and the lower foreign repercussions on exports which characterize smaller countries. Despite the lower multiplier, these same characteristics also mean that the net effect of the given autonomous change on the balance of trade is likely to be more adverse in smaller countries. Income-induced increases in imports, if unrestrained, may be a significant reversal factor in small countries. But these secondary income effects cannot eliminate the primary improvement in the balance of trade unless the home country's marginal propensity to spend exceeds unity, which is improbable.

Devaluation by a Small Nation

The second source of reversal lies in the secondary increases in the prices of traded goods. Direct price increases in the home country following devaluation have already been taken into account in the elasticities formulas, but there may be important indirect price increases. It is known that the extent of the direct price increases of traded goods depends on the trade elasticities, given the proportion of devaluation of the currency. (Of course, the smaller this proportion the smaller these price increases, *ceteris paribus*.) In brief, the rise in the domestic price of traded goods will be greater the greater the trade elasticities abroad (ϵ_f, η_f) and the lower the home elasticities of demand and supply (ϵ_h, η_h).[7] The reverse propositions apply to the world price of traded goods.

To the extent that small countries tend to face high elasticities abroad (ϵ_f, η_f) and to have inelastic home elasticities (ϵ_h, η_h), whereas the reverse is true of large countries, it follows that the direct increase in the domestic price of traded goods is likely to be greater than the increase in large countries. What effect these increases will have on the general price level of both traded and non-traded goods will depend on the ratio of traded goods to national absorption. If one assumes that the domestic prices of non-traded goods remain constant or increase less than the prices of traded goods, it is clear that the greater the share of traded goods in total absorption, the greater the increase in the general price level, for a given increase in the price of import and export goods. Indeed, the relative size of the foreign trade sector in relation to national absorption is probably more important than the extent of the direct price change of traded goods alone in determining the change in the general price level.[8] Chapter III contained comment on the high values of the ratio of trade to national absorption of both consumption and investment goods in small countries. Because of these high ratios and because of the high increases in the price of traded goods, a relatively great increase in the general price level in small countries can be expected.

A second source of rising prices is the multiplier process initiated by any primary improvement in the balance of trade. This process will be more inflationary if it occurs under conditions of full employment of resources. If there is a link between money wages and indices of the cost of living in the devaluing country, the money wages will rise in response to the increase in the cost of living and cause further increases in the price level of both traded and non-traded goods. These

---

7. Fleming, "Exchange Depreciation," p. 295; Alexander, "The Effects of Devaluation: A Synthesis," Appendix.
8. See Fleming, "Exchange Depreciation," pp. 298–301.

secondary increases will raise the costs of production in the export industries. To the extent that export products utilize imported factor components, the direct increases in import prices will also raise the domestic costs of producing these products.

For the above reasons concerning the price elasticities, the ratio of traded goods to national absorption, the marginal propensity to import, and foreign repercussions, it can be argued that reversal in the balance of trade may be greater in small countries than in large countries. Orcutt concluded on the grounds of the higher trade ratios and marginal propensities to import in small countries that "it is clear that the combined importance of the secondary repercussions also will be less when one large bloc depreciates relative to the rest of the world than when a small country depreciates against the rest of the world." [9]

However, these lines of reasoning, while possibly true in some cases, are purely conjectural. Indeed, nothing can be said about the precise nature of the "secondary" effects of devaluation unless the nature of the fiscal and monetary policies simultaneously pursued by the devaluing country are explicitly specified. For example, the effects of devaluation on the money supply and on national income via an increase in overseas assets of the banking system could possibly be important in small countries where these assets are a more significant part of the total assets of the banks. As Tsaing, Meade, Pearce, Kemp, and many others have demonstrated, there is such a widely divergent range of possible assumptions concerning the behavior of the money and government sectors that little can be said about the "secondary" effects other than that they will offset to some degree the favorable primary effects.

The tendency for the inflationary pressure to be greater in a small country than in a large country if unsuppressed, may be completely offset by a rigorous anti-inflationary policy. It has been suggested on one occasion that the cultural homogeneity of small nations may lead to a more enlightened political government. [1] If this be true, the case for devaluation as an effective cure of balance of payments deficits in small countries is a strong one. In this event, the foreign elasticities of demand and supply facing a small country, if high, will insure that the final effect on the balance of trade will be favorable; such is the case described by Fleming. Contrary to Orcutt, he concludes that in the final analysis devaluation is likely to be more effective in small than in large countries. This result occurs largely because his model is predicated explicitly on the premise that all countries automatically adopt a

---

9. Orcutt, "Exchange Rate Adjustment," p. 6.
1. See *Economic Consequences,* pp. 31, 209.

compensatory monetary and fiscal policy such that the desired level of aggregate employment remains unchanged after devaluation.

I conclude that the familiar a priori argument concerning a high elasticity of foreign demand for the exports of a small nation is not generally applicable. The primary effects of devaluation by a small nation may in some cases be sufficiently favorable to suggest this alternative but they will depend on the specific products exported by this country, their share of the foreign markets, the pattern of commodity concentration of these exports, and the other elasticities. Similarly the generalities that have been made relating to the adverse secondary effects of devaluation in a small country are by no means certain to apply to each small country. The sole advantage that all small countries clearly have over the large trading nations is that the risk of retaliation by other countries is low. (On the other hand, they may have to follow suit if one of their main trading partners devalues. For example, all the European and Sterling Area members of the group of fifteen small developed countries changed their exchange rates following the 1949 devaluation of pound sterling.)

The final effect of devaluation in a small (or large) country depends probably most of all upon the monetary and fiscal policies adopted at the time of devaluation. The possibility of successful revaluations is clearly indicated by the precedents of Austria in 1953, Finland in 1957, Israel in 1962, and also by the successful appreciations of the New Zealand pound in 1948 and the Dutch guilder in 1961. All the devaluations greatly improved the balance of trade of the devaluing countries.[2] Yet the advisability of devaluation always rests on the unique circumstances and the wisdom of the monetary and fiscal policies of the country contemplating this choice.

---

2. Though we should note that the percentage increases in the official domestic price of foreign currencies for the devaluations by Austria, Finland, and Israel (1962) were all large. They were, respectively, 22, 39, and 66 per cent.

CHAPTER VI

The Small Nation in a Graham Model of International Trade

From the time of J. S. Mill [1] to Frank Graham's "heretical" critique of Classical theory,[2] it was commonly supposed that the larger portion of the gains from a given volume of trade between any two trading countries accrued to the poorer of these two nations. This was supposed to result because the high level of demand of the rich country for the exports of the relatively poor country, together with the low level of demand of the poor country for the exports of the rich country, moved the ratio of exchange or the terms of trade toward the limiting pre-trade ratio of the rich country. Similarly, it was believed that in a multi-country world the terms of trade favored poor countries.[3] These propositions were accepted on faith by the Neoclassical economists down to Alfred Marshall.[4] In the discussions of these authors the terms "richness" and "poorness" appear to relate to per capita income.[5]

J. S. Nicholson specifically introduced the factor of size of nations in order to analyze more carefully the nature of bilateral trade. Indeed, he claimed that it was the omission of the factor of country size itself that had led to some confusion in Mill's statement.[6] It was Nicholson, and not Mill, who first stated the principle that if countries were not of approximately equal size, the terms of trade would settle at or near the comparative cost ratios of the larger of two countries.[7] The principle was reiterated by C. F. Bastable,[8] who considered trade between

---

1. J. S. Mill, *Principles of Political Economy*, ed. W. J. Ashley (new ed.; London, 1909), p. 604.
2. Frank Graham, "The Theory of International Values Re-examined," in *Readings in the Theory of International Trade*, pp. 301–330.
3. Mill, *Principles*, actually phrased his pioneer passage in terms of many countries. See also C. F. Bastable, *The Theory of International Trade* (4th ed., rev.; London, 1903), p. 43.
4. Alfred Marshall, *Money, Credit and Commerce* (London, 1923), chap. vii.
5. See Mill, *Principles*, p. 604; Marshall, *Money, Credit and Commerce*, pp. 168–169; Graham, "Theory of International Values Re-examined," p. 320.
6. J. Nicholson, *Principles of Political Economy*, 2 vols. (New York, 1897), II, 302, n. 2.
7. *Ibid.*, pp. 302–307.
8. *Theory of International Trade*, p. 43.

a small and a large country a "special case" of trade.[9] Nicholson (and Bastable and Graham after him) measured size in terms of product capacity. The measure of size in a Graham comparative advantage model will be discussed shortly. Marshall discussed briefly the case of many small and large countries trading.[1] He subscribed to Nicholson's views with some modifications, which related chiefly to the fact that in a many-country world, the large (or, vice versa, the small) nations traded with other large nations in addition to their trade with small nations.

Mill had recognized the possibility of an "extreme case" in which the post-trade price ratio settled at one of the countries' limiting pre-trade ratios, but he did not state the proposition in terms of the size of the countries. Admittedly, of two countries with similar populations, the one with the larger per capita income is in all probability the one with the larger product capacity. In this event the richer country is likely to be also the larger country in the Nicholson-Graham sense. Both Marshall and Graham treat large nations as the richer nations and small nations as the relatively poor nations.[2] Nevertheless, in view of the need for precision in trade models, it is preferable to define more precisely the characteristics of the nations involved.

Frank Graham later renewed Nicholson's contention that the introduction of the size factor is essential for an understanding of the international trade model.[3] Indeed, Graham on one occasion regarded the omission of this factor as a "great deficiency in classical theory."[4] In the case of the two countries, one small and one large, trading exclusively between themselves, Graham concluded, as had Nicholson before him, that the post-trade ratio of exchange for the two goods traded would settle at the limiting comparative advantage cost ratio of the large country. The whole of the gains from international trade

---

9. *Ibid.*, p. 179, n. 1. This Neoclassical proposition concerning the terms of trade between one large and one small country can be demonstrated by the use of Marshallian reciprocal demand curves. See Jacob Viner, *Studies in the Theory of International Trade* (New York, 1937), pp. 546–547, and T. M. Whitin, "Classical Theory, Graham's Theory and Linear Programming in International Trade," *Quarterly Journal of Economics,* LXVII (Nov., 1953), 528.

1. *Money, Credit and Commerce,* chap. vii. Marshall employs the absolute size of population rather than the product capacity as the criterion of national size (p. 170). See also Frank Graham's comment on Marshall in the former's *Theory of International Values,* pp. 236–237.

2. Marshall, *Money, Credit and Commerce,* pp. 168–170; Graham, *Theory of International Values,* p. 236 *et passim.*

3. Graham's writings on this subject are in three sources: "Theory of International Values Re-examined"; "The Theory of International Values," *Quarterly Journal of Economics,* XLVI (Aug., 1932), 581–616; and *Theory of International Values.*

4. *Theory of International Values,* p. 258.

would accrue to the small country. In order for both countries to gain from trade, they must be of approximately equal size.[5] By this they meant that the countries must be of approximately equal "productive" *and* "consuming" capacities. Graham writes of countries being of equal "economic importance" in this sense.[6] This notion of equal size in the sense of approximately equal productive and consuming capacities is somewhat vague and imprecise because size has been given two different dimensions. The analysis of the terms of trade of a small vis-à-vis a large country has often been equally imprecise.[7] The early examples chosen to illustrate the principle that small countries gain more from trade are extreme examples in which the productive power of the larger country is much greater than that of the small country. This disparity suffices to insure that the small country cannot supply the total demand of the two countries for the good it exports.[8] Hence the large country produces some quantity of both goods and specializes only partially. The terms of trade are most favorable to the small country. No precise measure of size is required in these simple illustrations.

In the two-country, two-good model, supply—which can be considered in terms of the capacities of the two countries to produce the two goods—and the demand conditions determine the equilibrium price ratio. A precise mathematical statement of the model shows that the price ratio is more likely to settle at the pre-trade limits of one country the greater the relative inequality in the size of the countries in terms of their productive capacities alone and the lower the elasticity of substitution in consumption.[9]

Graham's most important contribution in the area with which we are concerned was his finding that the effects of country size on the gains from trade and other features of the pattern of international trade in a many-country, many-product model conflict in some respects with the effects indicated by earlier writers who had relied upon the two-country, two-good model. In recent years Graham's many-country model of international trade has received more attention,

---

5. Graham, "Theory of International Values Re-examined," p. 303; Nicholson, *Principles,* pp. 302–304.
6. "Theory of International Values Re-examined," p. 314.
7. For example, Bastable, *Theory of International Trade,* p. 43, and Graham, "Theory of International Values Re-examined," pp. 304, 314.
8. See Nicholson, *Principles,* pp. 302–305, and Graham, "Theory of International Values Re-examined," p. 304, in his example of England and Denmark.
9. See the statement of the Graham model by John S. Chipman, "A Survey of the Theory of International Trade: Part I, The Classical Theory," *Econometrica,* XXXIII (July, 1965), 485–486, 491.

notably from Lionel McKenzie.[1] We shall see that the analytical properties of the Graham model allow the introduction of the factor of national size explicitly into the model of comparative advantage when size is defined in a particular way. Indeed, the Graham model is particularly important because it is the only many-country, many-good model of comparative advantage in which the (pre-trade) size of countries has been introduced as a variable, and it yields significant results.

In the many-country, many-good model, the definition of country size presents many more difficulties than in the two-country, two-good model. Caves, in his survey of international trade theory, notes that international trade theorists "have frequently assumed that demand patterns are the same or similar in all countries" and that "only sporadically" have they imputed "an active role to demand in determining international equilibrium."[2] Graham follows this procedure in his generalized model.

On the supply side the obvious measure of country size is that of product capacity. This method of measuring size was implicit in the earlier Neoclassical treatments of national size in their models of comparative advantage. Nicholson, for example, in considering the case in which two countries are of "equal size," assumes that both countries could produce equal amounts of the two goods, cloth and wheat.[3] T. M. Whitin, in his graphical exposition of the multi-country, two-good Graham model, relaxes the requirement that countries of equal size must produce equal amounts of both goods.[4] He measures the size of the countries by the length of their linear production transformation curves, or—what is the same thing—by the length of the line segments on the world transformation curve. This easy solution is not possible in the case of more than two goods. In this case, instead of a two-dimensional line representing the locus of all optimum

---

1. McKenzie's work is contained in three articles: "Specialisation and Efficiency in World Production," *Review of Economic Studies*, XII, No. 3 (1953-1954), 156-157; "Specialisation in Production and the Production Possibility Locus," *Review of Economic Studies*, XXIII, No. 1 (1955–1956), 56–64; "On Equilibrium in Graham's Model of World Trade and Other Competitive Systems," *Econometrica*, XII (April, 1954), 147–161.

The latest statement of the mathematical properties of Graham's model is that by John Chipman, "A Survey of the Theory of International Trade: Part I," principally pp. 493–501. Unfortunately, neither McKenzie nor Chipman was concerned with the size of countries, except insofar as size is a factor affecting the tendency toward partial specialization and limiting commodity price ratios. They do not pursue Graham's other suggestions concerning the pattern of trade of small nations.

2. Caves, *Trade and Economic Structure*, p. 205.
3. *Principles*, p. 306.
4. "Classical Theory," p. 528.

production possibilities in a country, there is a multi-dimensional surface of production possibilities.

Graham used the concept of product capacity as an index of "economic importance" in his general many-country, many-good model. In his early exposition of the three-good, four-country model, however, he had to resort to the production possibility of one good, cloth, as the index of product capacity and national size in a many-good world.[5] He followed the same convention in his later book.[6] For any post-trade set of commodity exchange ratios this criterion exaggerates the true relative size (in a general sense of capacity to produce the many goods) of those countries that have a comparative advantage in the production of the particular good selected as the index, and it correspondingly understates the size of all other countries. Nevertheless, in the absence of a sophisticated mathematical measure of the multi-dimensional surface, this is the only common basis by which the size of a country in the sense of product capacity can be measured.

No attempt is made here to explain the operation of a Graham model; this explanation has already been accomplished by other writers.[7] Graham's own observations in various places on small nations, however, are collated and discussed following a brief outline of the model. The following are the principal features of Graham's trade models and the later activity analysis models inspired by his early work. There are many countries and many final products. There is a single primary factor of production called "units of productive power" or sometimes simply "labor." In each country, the total endowment or supply of the primary factor is regarded as fixed initially and unchanging. This constrains the production and trade possibilities of each nation. Further, in all activities there are constant opportunity costs which are generally different in each country, and it is possible to produce the outputs of final products in any proportion. These supply conditions are strictly Classical. The essential and important difference between Graham's and prior statements of the Classical

---

5. "Theory of International Values Re-examined," p. 315.
6. *Theory of International Values*, p. 90, n. 2, and p. 76, n. 2.
7. The geometric presentation worked out by Whitin is particularly helpful ("Classical Theory"). Using his geometrical version of Graham's model he obtains the same conclusions concerning size of country and international trade as does Graham. Graham's feat in generalizing his relatively complex model to many countries solely with the aid of crude numerical examples is truly extraordinary. While McKenzie was preoccupied with the existence of an equilibrium and related matters, rather than with the effects of country size in his Graham model, his results verify the susceptibility of smaller countries to changes in their terms of trade ("Specialisation and Efficiency," p. 176).

model is that he dealt explicitly with a model of many countries and many goods.

The Classical assumption of given quantities of the one primary factor in each country is obviously unrealistic. But this assumption, together with that of constant productivities of this factor in each activity, merely serves to determine each country's production possibilities for all final products. As an alternative, one may assume that all countries have fixed opportunity costs over all ranges of production of all products and fixed supplies of all factors. This pair of assumptions produces the same multi-dimensional production possibility surface and the same results as do Graham's assumptions.

On the demand side, Graham, following J. S. Mill, assumed that in each country a constant proportion of domestic income is expended on each of the given number of commodities, regardless of income and prices, an assumption which implies that all demand functions have unit price and income elasticities. Graham also assumes at times that the proportions are each equal in all countries, which conveniently implies that the proportion of world income devoted to each product is constant and unaffected by any redistribution of world income among countries. For simplicity alone, he makes a third assumption that the proportions spent on the various products are themselves equal. As McKenzie proved, such restrictive assumptions concerning the demand functions are not necessary in a Graham model.[8] Moreover, the assumption of fixed consumption proportions had an important effect on Graham's results and his stress on the size factor, for it implies unitary elasticities of substitution among all goods in consumption. This apparently innocent assumption, made for convenience, removed the influence of variations in the elasticity of substitution, which is the second factor in a general Graham model that affects the likelihood of partial specialization and "limbo" or limit price ratios.[9]

Employing the definition of size in terms of the capacity to produce

---

8. McKenzie, "Specialisation and Efficiency," pp. 156–157. On the supply side McKenzie generalized the Graham model so that there may be any number of ultimate factors, costs are not necessarily constant, the production of intermediate products is allowed, and factor supplies and factor proportions are variable. The significance of McKenzie's extensions can be appreciated when one considers that he has many factors with variable proportions, yet he has not introduced the Ohlin assumption of identical production functions for all goods in all countries or the implied assumption that each country possesses some quantity of all of an identical set of factors.

9. See Chipman, "A Survey of the Theory of International Trade: Part I," for a precise statement of this aspect of a Graham model.

one product, Graham examined the historic proposition that small countries gain more from trade than large countries with more careful analysis than any of his predecessors.[1] In a multi-country, multi-good world, it is the total world demand and supply—and not that of any two countries that may exchange a certain internationally-traded good—that determine the final exchange ratios. A large country cannot completely specialize in the product in which it enjoys the greatest comparative advantage since after a partial specialization in the production of this good the world exchange ratios of this good for other goods will be reduced to the potential exchange ratios of the large country. Many of the goods a large country exports will exchange for imports at the same ratios as its own potential or actual opportunity cost ratios. Its gains from trade are therefore greatly reduced, though positive gain still exists from other goods it imports.

Conversely, Graham's own model does substantiate the Neoclassical claim that small nations obtain greater gains per unit of trade. But his model reveals that in a many-country world the real advantage of small countries lies in their ability to specialize exclusively in a few goods in which they enjoy a great comparative advantage. Their gains are typically greater because of the typical great difference between the production transformation ratios at which they can produce all goods themselves and the world price ratios at which they can obtain the goods, not because of their low level of demand for the goods of the larger countries, as the Classical economists contended.[2] These cost differences represent the sole way in which a small country tends to benefit more from trade than a large country.[3] (Incidentally, Graham, like the earlier Classical economists, believed that large gains from trade would accrue to "poor" countries for the same reason. He regarded these countries as "a special case of the question of size.")[4]

Small countries exhibit other closely related characteristics in a Graham model of many countries and many goods. One feature is that the exports of a small country tend to be more concentrated than the

---

1. For Graham's views on country size and the pattern of international trade, see especially "Theory of International Values Re-examined," p. 315, and *Theory of International Values*, pp. 58-59, 235-241.

2. See also Whitin, "Classical Theory," p. 535. For an example of a two-country, four-good case in which the large country produces all four goods and receives no gain from trade, see Graham, *Theory of International Values*, p. 171.

3. However, in a multi-country world, in which small and large countries may obtain the imports of the same good from several different countries, and more than one import good is exchanged for the goods exported, the notion of gains from trade becomes ambiguous; see Graham, *Theory of International Values*, chap. xi.

4. *Ibid.*, p. 242.

exports of a large country. This feature arises partly because of the more limited productive capacities of these countries and partly because of the greater probabilities that small countries will have a smaller range of potential products whose opportunity cost ratios are more widely dispersed than those of large nations. Most small countries, possessing a small productive capacity in relation to world demand for these products, are able to specialize in the production of those goods in which they enjoy a great comparative advantage. (Other a priori reasons for expecting this feature of the international trade of small countries and the empirical evidence were examined in Chapter II.)

In the multi-country, multi-good Graham model the post-trade commodity exchange ratios are predominantly determined by the supply conditions of the larger countries. "This means that, over a considerable range of products, the cost ratios in a large country will be the same as the exchange ratios in the world at large and will, in fact, determine them." [5] Certain consequences follow from this feature of the Graham model. One consequence is the manner in which a shift in the world demand from one commodity to another commodity may affect the terms of trade of small and large countries. In the Graham model small shifts in demand among commodities will not in general affect the commodity exchange ratios. There will, however, be compensating adjustments in the quantity supplied by various countries and in particular by the larger suppliers of the commodities affected. Consider the case of small countries which are able to specialize in the production of a single good which is also produced by some other (larger) countries. Such small countries are not affected in any way by a shift in world demand if this shift is insufficient to alter the ratios at which these products exchange in the world market for other products. Their income, their terms of trade, and, moreover, their total production and export of the good are unchanged. The only adjustment is in the supply of the same good by the larger country or countries which also produce this good.[6]

The limits to the extent of the shift of demand among commodities that will not alter the international exchange ratios are also determined in part by the size of the countries producing the commodities affected by this change.[7] The larger the producing countries concerned, the greater the extent to which they can expand or contract their

---

5. *Ibid.*, p. 235.
6. Graham illustrates this proposition and most of the others discussed in this section by means of arithmetic examples (*ibid.*, chaps. vi-vii).
7. *Ibid.*, p. 108.

supplies of these commodities in response to a change in demand—with corresponding contractions or expansions of the other goods they produce—without altering the international exchange ratios. In the case above in which a small country is only one among several suppliers of its export good, there may be large shifts of demand for this product without affecting the world exchange ratios because of the supply adjustments in the larger countries. But if all countries producing the goods for which the demand is assumed to change are relatively small, there is more likely to be a change in the international exchange ratios. (Shifts in supply by other countries—especially other large countries—that also produce products exported by small countries may have similar consequences.)

However, in the event of a large shift of demand (or supply) that does cause a change in world exchange ratios of goods traded by a small country, such a small country is more susceptible to significant changes in its terms of trade and real income than are large countries.[8] The reason is that small nations with a limited productive capacity will tend to have fewer potential exports and a greater range in the comparative costs of these goods than larger countries. Hence a given shift in the exchange ratios causes a greater change in the comparative advantage of goods now exported, the pattern of production, and the terms of trade on which small countries may obtain their imports, than it will for large countries. Large countries whose actual and potential exports are more diversified are much less affected by such shifts in commodity exchange ratios.

In the rare case in which a small country engages in the production of a single good which is not produced by another country, the slightest change in the demand for this good will affect the commodity exchange ratios and the terms of trade for this country. This happens because there can be no compensating adjustments of supply elsewhere.[9] For similar reasons, a small country which concentrates its production on a few goods only may suffer a decline in real income if the per capita productivity rises in these industries.[1] This decline will occur if the country consumes little of these home-produced goods itself and is thus precluded from benefiting directly from the increased productivity and if there are no large countries which produce these goods. This latter circumstance precludes the adjustment or decrease in supply in these other countries that would obviate the deteriora-

---

8. *Ibid.*, pp. 135-136.
9. *Ibid.*, p. 114, n. 1; *et passim.*
1. *Ibid.*, pp. 212-213.

tion in the small country's terms of trade. This deterioration of the terms of trade and national income of the small country will also be aggravated if there are no other potential export goods in this small country whose comparative advantage ratios are close to the ratio of the good or goods initially exported. This is Graham's version—and it is a carefully worked out version—of the old Classical problem of what is today called "immiserising growth" due to (Hicks-neutral) technical change.[2]

Graham is careful to indicate that these characteristics are not certain to apply to all small countries; they are merely more probable the smaller the country because of the behavior of his many-country model. A small country unfortunate enough not to possess at least one export whose opportunity costs differ markedly from those in other countries will not enjoy large gains from trade. Conversely, a small country fortunate enough to have potential export goods other than those actually traded in which it enjoys a substantial comparative advantage, will not be greatly harmed by a fall in the world prices of its actual exports.

Finally, one may presume, though Graham does not discuss this aspect, that these same factors will tend to imply that small countries have a higher ratio of exports and imports of goods and services to national product than large countries. This tendency exists simply because small countries tend to specialize to a greater extent in the production of goods for export in exchange for the products they do not produce themselves.

Graham's model assumes an adaptability of quantities and numbers of products produced and exported in all countries that does not exist, in the short run at least. Yet his model is most instructive. It clearly indicates that the tendency for small countries to enjoy greater gains from international trade, by virtue of their greater specialization in a few goods and their susceptibility to changes in the terms of trade and real incomes when the basic world demand or supply conditions alter, are joint results of the smaller and more limited range of production in these countries. These tendencies only apply *ceteris paribus*. As observed in Chapter II the size of countries is only one of very many factors that determine the actual patterns of international trade, and its influence is often swamped by location, trade barriers, and other considerations from which the Graham model and most other comparative advantage models abstract completely.

---

2. Chipman, "A Survey of the Theory of International Trade: Part I," p. 490, provides a list of references to the Classical discussions of this problem.

CHAPTER VII

Economies of Scale, Country Size, and Customs Unions

I

Arguments about the extent of the market to which industries have access and the possibilities of realizing economies of scale are at once the most familiar and the most unsatisfactory of all arguments on the implications of national size. The two principal reasons these debates have been so unsatisfactory are, first, the unclear relationships between the size of the economy on the one hand and economies of scale and the pattern of production and international trade on the other and second, the absence of empirical studies on the critical aspects of size and trade. I have already touched on economies of scale and national size as a determinant of trade patterns in Chapter II and of the rate of growth in Chapter III. In neither of these cases did national size appear to be a major influence. This chapter is concerned with economies of scale and the effect on a small developed country of joining a customs union or free trade area containing a larger country or larger countries. Membership in a free trade area will have much the same effects in this respect as membership in a customs union since both imply completely free trade among member countries.

This chapter is to a greater extent than the previous ones a survey of the literature and ideas, with less pretense to originality. I shall, however, approach the theory of customs unions from the point of view of the possible effects on a single prospective member country alone rather than from the customary point of view of gains and losses to the union as a whole, for a country contemplating membership in a union is principally concerned with the effects of union on its own economy. It is remarkable how little has been written on the effects of union on individual member countries. After surveying the writings on small developed countries and their short-run problems in joining customs unions or free trade areas in Section II, I shall in Section III discuss the long-run problems, in particular the dangers of the polarization of industries in larger countries. In Section IV there are some comments on the experiences to date of small developed countries which are members of actual unions or free trade areas. Section V emphasizes the parallels between the concerns of small developed countries and the rapidly growing literature on trade liberalization and the developing countries. In all sections, I shall concentrate on the effects of union on the pattern of production in member countries, especially in decreasing cost manufacturing industries, leaving aside such issues as the effects of union on the terms of trade and on the balance of payments.

II

Before discussing economies of scale and customs unions I shall dispose of some other aspects of country size and customs union theory. Most of the analysis of the Viner-Meade type of static effects of customs unions proceeds explicitly or implicitly on the basis that the union is of states of any size or that the size of the individual members does not affect the outcome of the union. There has, however, been some comment on the aggregate size of the union as a factor that determines its effects on trade creation and diversion and therefore on the welfare of the union and the rest of the world. Several well-known generalizations follow, assuming either constant or increasing marginal costs and perfect competition in all industries.[1] Perhaps the most important is that the welfare of the union as a whole, and of the world, is greater the more competitive or similar are member countries in terms of the list of tradable commodities produced by members before union and the more complementary or dissimilar they are in terms of the spread of member countries' production costs of these commodities. As Viner[2] and many others subsequently have stated, this source of gain from "production effects" will tend to be greater the greater the aggregate size of the union, other things being equal. (Most of the commentators are not precise in their definition of union size. The most suitable definition here appears to be that of productive capacity or in practice national income, despite the small circularity involved in using the latter, which is a post-trade magnitude, to predict

---

1. These generalizations are very ably surveyed by R. G. Lipsey, "The Theory of Customs Unions: A General Survey," *Economic Journal,* LXX (Sept., 1960), 498–513.

2. Jacob Viner, *The Customs Union Issue* (New York, 1951), pp. 51, 135; "Customs unions are unlikely to yield more economic benefit than harm unless they are between sizeable countries which practice substantial protection of substantially similar industries. But customs unions of this character have always been extremely difficult to negotiate in a nationalistic and protectionist world" (p. 135). The last comment is quite pertinent to at least one contemporary agreement, Latin American Free Trade Area (LAFTA), which has not had much success in exchanging concessions on important substantially-protected industries.

the effects of increased trade.) Jan Tinbergen employs a formal model in which he varies the size of the union by increasing the number of countries of equal size to show that the larger the aggregate size of the union the larger the increase in the welfare of the union and the world as a whole.[3] Another proposition is that the larger the proportion of the total pre-union international trade of members which is conducted with future members, the greater the prospects for trade creation and the smaller the prospects for trade diversion.

Little attention has been paid to the effect of the size of the individual member country on its own static gains or losses from membership in a union. Fundamentally, the static gains to a country from union will be larger the larger, of course, the trade creation occurring in a member's export or import trade and the smaller the trade diversion in its import trade. For the same reasons as given for the aggregate size of the union, it would seem that the larger the size of an individual country in a multi-country union the larger its total net gains from joining the union are likely to be. This effect will occur to the extent that larger countries will tend to produce and be able to export a greater range of internationally tradable products that are also produced before union by other members, other things being equal. Larger members may also be harmed less by imports of trade-diverted products from other members. There is an additional and probably less important factor that may favor some large countries: from the point of view of the static "consumption effects," it can be shown that "the sort of countries who ought to form customs unions are those doing a high proportion of their foreign trade with their union partners and making a high proportion of their total expenditure on domestic trade."[4]

In recent writings, however, the main concern has been with the "dynamic" and long-run effects of a union. If a union increases the degree of competition in industries, it provides the incentive for firms to adopt more efficient methods of production and eliminates marginal high-cost producers. Some authors have stressed these benefits for small member countries.[5] Gains from increased competition will depend on the establishment of effective competition after union, and they are probably most important in industries subject to decreasing costs. Some possible gain to large and small members alike may also

---

3. "Customs Unions: Influence of Their Size on Their Effect," pp. 404–414.
4. Lipsey, "The Theory of Customs Unions," pp. 507–509.
5. Scitovsky, in *Economic Consequences*, pp. 282–290, and Edwards, in *ibid.*, pp. 117–130.

accrue because of improved terms of trade vis-à-vis the rest of the world and better bargaining power of the union bloc in international trade negotiations. But the most important "dynamic" effect is usually considered to be the effects of union on production in industries subject to decreasing costs. Economists dealing with the effects of customs unions on developing countries have also shared this preoccupation. The rest of this section is devoted to the effects of trade liberalization among a group of countries on the production of goods in decreasing-cost industries.

In the same way that the static theory of customs unions and free trade areas uses the model of comparative advantage under completely free trade as a standard of comparison, it may be instructive to look at the pattern of trade when some industries are subject to decreasing costs under the same conditions of unrestricted free trade. This was done in Chapter II, but the sole prediction it yielded was that small countries may produce some—but a more limited number of—products in decreasing-cost industries than may larger countries. The very smallness of these countries' productive capacities will restrict the output of goods requiring large-scale production. For the products in which a small country specializes, access to the markets of foreign countries enables it to escape at least some of the limitations of the smallness of its own markets and to realize economies of scale; however, protective trade barriers and the risks of foreign trade restrict access to the markets of other countries. In contrast to the pure theory of comparative advantage, the discussions of the effects of forming a customs union in a protectionist world on the production of goods in decreasing-cost industries can claim to have at least inquired into the main determinants of international trade in these goods. We shall see that the nature of competition and the degree of product differentiation are important determinants of international trade within a union.

Probably the first explicit treatment of small nations and the effects on them of joining regional economic groupings was that of the Austrian economist K. W. Rothschild in 1944.[6] Rothschild argued that a small nation may be adversely affected if it enters a union which includes a larger country. His argument turns on the existence before the union in each country of some monopolistic or oligopolistic industries producing close substitute goods. In the event of a mutual

---

6. K. W. Rothschild, "The Small Nation and World Trade," *Economic Journal*, LIV (April, 1944), 26–40. He later restated much the same argument in "Kleinstaat und Integration," *Weltwirtschaftliches Archiv*, No. 2 (1963), pp. 239–273.

reduction of tariff barriers, the smaller monopolistic producers in the industries of the smaller of two or more countries will, he contended, in all likelihood be eliminated because the larger producer in the larger country has the larger financial reserves. Production in the smaller country after union may be limited to small-scale industries and agriculture.[7] This is a very inadequate argument. Nevertheless, Rothschild's concern for the fate of industries in small countries was prophetic of some recent debate to which we shall return later.

Tibor Scitovsky was the first to provide a comprehensive and careful analysis of international specialization and the effect of the formation of a customs union when there are decreasing costs in some industries.[8] For industries in which the cost curves are U-shaped and there is a unique long-run optimum or least-cost scale of production, he makes a most useful distinction between two possible explanations of why firms in small countries may operate at sub-optimal capacity.[9] The first explanation is that the economy is "technologically" too small. By this he means that the markets are too small to support even one optimum-scale plant operating at full capacity. Domestic production of a product subject to increasing returns will only cease completely, however, if the market for that product is so small that not even one single producer acting as a perfectly discriminating monopolist can secure what is considered an adequate profit on the capital invested. The second explanation of production at a sub-optimal scale is that the economy may be "economically" too small. This occurs when the market size is large enough to provide a profitable outlet for the least-cost production of at least one optimum-sized plant, but too small in terms of total expenditure to be able to provide a domestic outlet for a number of firms producing at this rate of output. In the absence of a sufficient number of producers, monopolistic producers maximize profits at less-than-optimum outputs. This means that they may instal either a sub-optimal scale of plant from the long-run point of view or that they install the most efficient equipment but operate it at less than optimum capacity. The size of the economy required to provide effective and efficient competition may be consider-

---

7. "The Small Nation and World Trade," p. 31.
8. "Economies of Scale, Competition, and European Integration," *American Economic Review*, XLVI (March, 1956), 71–91. This essay is reproduced and the analysis further pursued in *Economic Theory and West European Integration* (Stanford, 1958), chaps. i and iii; also, "International Trade and Economic Integration as a Means of Overcoming the Disadvantages of a Small Nation," in *Economic Consequences*, pp. 282–290.
9. *Economic Theory*, p. 113, and in *Economic Consequences*, pp. 282–283.

ably larger than the size necessary from the technological point of view.[1]

Scitovsky stated that only "in a few industries" were the markets of European countries too small "technologically." But he believed that the small economies were not large enough "economically" to provide effective competition. "I suspect, however, that in the great majority of Western Europe's manufacturing industries, the size of the actual or potential market is not the factor that prevents the exploitation of economies of scale." [2] Rather, exploitation of economies of scale is prevented by the coexistence of many small non-competitive, non-standardized, small-turnover, and high-profit-margin firms; in short, to the general absence of competitive behavior. Others have contended that many of the industries of small nations are highly monopolistic and therefore operate at less than optimum efficiency.[3] (Lack of competition may also result in super-optimal scales of production, but presumably this aspect of the problem is uncommon in small countries.) There are also indirect influences which may tend to make large economies more competitive. It is said that large countries are more diverse culturally and that business in these countries is less personalized and competition is therefore more effective.[4]

In the case of continuously decreasing costs, the economies of scale can never be fully exhausted in an economy of any size.[5] One producer (the first?) may supply the entire market. The limit to the expansion of the firm lies in the size of the market.

Most authors concerned with the trade of small (and developing) countries assume that the protective trade barriers and risks of foreign markets are such that international trade does not greatly increase the size of the markets of producers in these countries. These international trade barriers and risks prevent the realization of economies of scale in decreasing-cost industries.[6] Does membership in a customs union

---

1. *Economic Consequences*, p. 283.
2. *Economic Theory*, pp. 24–25.
3. Edwards, in *Economic Consequences*, p. 122; Marsan, in *ibid.*, pp. 159–162; Franz Gehrels and Bruce F. Johnston, "The Economic Gains of European Integration," *Journal of Political Economy*, LXIII (Aug., 1955), 282; Balassa, *Theory of Economic Integration*, pp. 167–169.
4. Edwards, in *Economic Consequences*, p. 127; Scitovsky, in *ibid.*, p. 285, and *Economic Theory*, chap. i.
5. Stephen Hymer and Peter Pashigian, "Firm Size and Rate of Growth," *Journal of Political Economy*, LXX (Dec., 1962), 556–569, give evidence of continual economies of scale in some United States manufacturing industries.
6. Marcy, in *Economic Consequences*, pp. 27–72; Triffin, in *ibid.*, pp. 248–252; Scitovsky, in *ibid.*, p. 284.

and access to its protection-free markets give small nations a second line of escape from smallness and sub-optimal scales of production?

In this section I shall consider the effect of the union on the utilization of *existing* industrial capacity only. Such utilization will depend largely on the type of competition among firms of all member nations that prevails after the union is formed. Any union will increase the number of competitors having unrestricted access to the whole union market, but Scitovsky in particular stresses that the number of firms alone does not determine the nature of competition.[7] If the national markets are competitive before the union then the union is likely to increase the degree of competition further. If the pre-union markets are monopolistic or oligopolistic, the freeing of trade "may lead to the displacement of national monopolies and oligopolies by European oligopolies and such a change need neither increase competition nor improve productive organization and efficiency."[8] Others have advanced this view,[9] but Scitovsky adds that union may on the other hand establish competition and break up cartels. "Which is the more likely occurrence one cannot tell on general grounds."[1] One factor that may contribute much toward increased competition is a less benevolent attitude on the part of union bodies toward restrictive pricing and output policies than the attitudes prevailing under separate governments.[2] The less personal nature of multi-country competition may have a similar effect.[3]

If the union increases the degree of competition, it provides an incentive to adopt a more efficient utilization of existing capacity and it provides the opportunities in the form of an access to duty-free union-wide markets. There may also be improvements in the methods of production and efficiency in factor use apart from the greater use of large-scale plant. If competition does increase, the gains from internal economies of scale will depend on the extent of these economies. Most of those writing on economies of scale and small countries merely presume that significant unexploited economies exist in a number of manufacturing industries. Curiously, many of the earlier writers were highly critical of this view that customs unions would lead to economies of large-scale production. Jacob Viner declared, "It does not seem probable that the prospects of reduction of unit costs of produc-

---

7. *Economic Theory,* pp. 25–28, and in *Economic Consequences,* pp. 285–286.
8. *Economic Theory,* p. 20.
9. Rothschild, "The Small Nation and World Trade"; Sydney Dell, *Trade Blocs and Common Markets* (New York, 1963), pp. 72–75.
1. *Economic Theory,* p. 20. Cf. Balassa, *Theory of Economic Integration,* chap. viii, who cites other views on the effects of union on competition.
2. Scitovsky, *Economic Theory,* p. 21.
3. *Ibid.,* pp. 25–28, and *Economic Consequences,* pp. 285–286.

tion as a result of enlargement of the tariff area are ordinarily substantial, even when the individual member countries are quite small in economic size." [4] The consensus at the 1957 Lisbon conference favored the skeptical view. In his summary of the proceedings E. A. G. Robinson noted: "Outside of a few exceptional industries most technical economies are exhausted by firms of quite moderate size. Even relatively small and poor countries can have a number of firms of the minimum size to give full, or almost full, technical efficiency." [5] At the outset one should note that there are certain industries whose unit costs are not likely to be affected by the scale of output. One category is the extractive industries located near raw materials; another category includes some products of superior technical quality that require skilled workmanship. Switzerland provides the classic example in the watch and precision instrument and machinery industries which are carried on by small firms, mass production methods being almost totally absent.

The empirical evidence concerning economies of scale in manufacturing industries is vast but contradictory and inconclusive. Most of it is provided by studies of productivity per worker, using cross-country or time series data. The validity of interpreting productivity differences as a measure of economies of scale is known to be doubtful. Bela Balassa has provided a useful survey of productivity studies. On the basis of data from several countries, he concludes that "as a general proposition, we can establish the presence of a positive correlation between plant size and productivity in a number of industries." [6] In the case of EEC he thought it would make exploitation of economies of scale possible for a number of industries. In his more recent study he foresees economies of scale in a number of industries within the Latin American Free Trade Area.[7]

Another widely quoted study is that by Hollis B. Chenery. He finds market size to be a significant determinant of the development of the manufacturing sector and of certain industries in particular. He gives an illustration of the "size" effect, holding per capita incomes constant at three hundred dollars: "An increase in population from 2 to 50 million causes manufacturing output per capita to nearly double and the sectors having significant economies of scale to more than triple. Beyond some point, market size should have less effect, but at the income level of $300 chosen here, economies of scale are probably

---

4. *The Customs Union Issue*, p. 46.
5. *Economic Consequences*, p. xvii.
6. *Theory of Economic Integration*, p. 131.
7. *Economic Development and Integration* (Mexico City, 1965), chap. iv.

significant up to a population of 100 million or more in most of these industries (a market equal to about 10 million people at U.S. income levels) ." [8] Using population as a measure of market size while holding per capita incomes constant understates the increase in market size in terms of national product and the effect of economies of scale. We should also note that this statistical association between the output per capita of manufacturing industries and population may be partly due to external economies of scale and increasing product specialization and to other factors as well as to internal economies of scale. The industries having significant size elasticities or "economies of scale" in his study included Metals, Machinery, Transport Equipment, and Chemicals.

To the extent that they do occur, we can at least be sure that economies of scale and improved methods of production resulting from increased competition will benefit the union as a whole. But will they harm or benefit small members of a union? As with the static theory, much less attention has been paid to gains or losses accruing to individual members than to those accruing to the union as a whole. Producers in all member countries have free access to the markets of all members; essentially the question is whether small countries will gain more from this access than they lose from increased competition at home and in member countries' markets. If there is aggressive competition among firms of different countries after union, the firms in small countries must produce at close to the same unit cost as the firms of the larger member countries to keep their markets within the free trade area.

In order to assess the impact on the industries of a small nation contemplating membership in a regional bloc, it is essential to assess the extent of economies of scale in the specific lines of production that these countries actually do or could produce with their given factor endowments. More exactly one would need to compare the unit costs of production of members in these industries. There are many complications. Prior reasoning does not imply that the scale of production of plants in small countries will always be smaller than that in the same industries of larger countries. However, we can expect this to be so in many cases, especially if the differences in country size are great.[9] Furthermore, there is no certainty that the plants of smaller countries will have higher unit costs even if they do have a smaller plant size in industries operating under decreasing costs. First, the actual unit

---

8. "Patterns of Industrial Growth," pp. 645–646.
9. By a plant here I mean the unit of production for a single product. Actual size of firms and "plants" tends to be increased in small countries because the firms produce several products. See sec. iii, below.

costs of individual plants, which is what matters in this context, depend on the particular shape of the cost function and the actual dispersion of plant sizes. Scitovsky did not foresee much reallocation of existing production among the countries of Western Europe upon union because there did not appear to be much variation in costs between countries.[1] Indeed, the evidence suggested that the cost differences were as great within countries as they were among producers of different countries. If the low-cost domestic producers have excess capacity, it is they, he claimed, rather than the foreign competitors who are likely to capture the market of the less efficient producers in a country. This situation existed in Europe because the pre-union size of the economies was large enough to support several firms but not large enough to provide effective competition. In some industries at least the lowest-cost producers in small countries appeared not to be at a disadvantage vis-à-vis producers in the larger countries. With Continental West Europe in mind Scitovsky, Marcy, and Triffin, in their papers at the Lisbon conference, advocated the formation of tariff-free areas as an escape from smallness and sub-optimal scales of production for both small and large European countries.

In comparing industries among different countries many factors other than the size of plant affect costs. These factors include methods of production, the specialization of plants by commodity, the presence of external economies, the degree of protection before the union, and, perhaps most important in some instances, the "unfashionable" explanation of individual efficiency and hard work.[2] Some of these factors may favor producers in small countries and mitigate the dangers of union to their producers. Marcy asserted that most industries of small countries which are highly engaged in international trade are less protected and may hence be more efficient than the firms of the same industries in large nations. "If this really proved to be so, the small nation's firm could get off to a good start and immediately draw ahead by a few lengths."[3] P. J. Verdoorn estimated that the descending order of countries according to their weighted average level of import duties in Europe in 1952 coincided almost exactly with the descending order by size of population.[4] Marcy raised another factor

---

1. *Economic Theory*, pp. 20-22.
2. *Economic Consequences*, p. xvi.
3. *Ibid.*, p. 273.
4. Cited by Scitovsky, *Economic Theory*, p. 76. Scitovsky used this correlation to indicate a second possible source of gain to smaller countries. After union the balance of payments of lower-tariff members could be expected to improve, and if their currencies were appreciated this would be likely to improve their intra-member terms of trade (*Economic Theory*, p. 49).

when he concluded that "all in all, we can perhaps say that a small nation's industry which produces specialized and high-quality products for which there is a great demand has every prospect of improving its position and expanding its markets within the free trade area." He added the proviso that "further expansion may in the future be held up by lack of capital and, above all, by lack of skilled labour." [5] These authors had only the European small countries in mind; the same factors may not favor other small countries participating in a customs union.

Still other factors reduce the danger of increased competition to some producers in small countries. To the extent that the economies of member nations are complementary rather than competitive in the goods they produce, there is no danger of small countries' industries being eliminated by more efficient competition. When one takes into account product differentiation for many goods, the degree of competitiveness in this respect may be greatly reduced. Studies referred to in Section IV indicate that product differentiation has been largely responsible for the small amount of industry dislocation and the large increases in intra-area trade for EEC and EFTA. In cases in which members do produce some of the same products, as Scitovsky emphasized,[6] the scope for short-term reallocation of production from plant existing at the time of the formation or joining of a union is limited by the amount of excess capacity and labor skills in the more efficient plants. This reallocation will not occur unless the low-cost producers have unused capacity to encroach upon their high-cost competitors and then only if the market after union is competitive. After union some industries may still have an oligopolistic or monopolistic structure. A small number of producers in some industries may find it profitable to allow the firms in small nations to continue production even if their unit costs are higher than those of the producers in large countries.

These factors of course do not mean that producers in some industries in small countries may not be at a cost disadvantage vis-à-vis producers in larger countries and stand to lose some of their sales after union. If other things are equal, the cost disadvantages of a small country are likely to be greatest when the small country before union has only one or a few producers in an industry, the optimal scale of production is large, and production in a small country cannot exhaust the economies of scale. What the qualifying factors do illustrate

---

5. *Economic Consequences*, p. 274.
6. *Economic Theory*, pp. 20–22.

is that the smallness of their home markets does not necessarily mean that small country producers in decreasing-cost industries will have a cost disadvantage. There is no simple connection between any of the above factors and the size of the country in terms of its aggregate output. The effects of union membership of small nations on their industries may be expected to differ according to the individual circumstances of the countries.

There is no presumption that all or most of the manufacturing output of small countries will be eliminated by cheaper competition from producers in larger countries. Only a detailed investigation of these factors in the particular industries of prospective members will give an indication of the extent of the likely changes, and the author knows of no such studies. In the absence of such empirical work all discussion of economies of scale and changes in the distribution of production of decreasing-cost industries within a customs union is speculation, at best enlightened speculation.

III

In Section II, attention was restricted to the short-run effects on the reallocation of *existing* industry capacities. According to Scitovsky the utilization of existing capacity is less significant than the allocation of *new* post-union investment funds.[7] Scitovsky attempts to assess the likely effects of union on investment possibilities.[8] But there are so many imponderables that affect this allocation in the long run, such as the degree of competition in industries after union, the rate of accretion of demand to each industry as income levels rise and demand patterns shift, the exchange rates established, and industrial policies, that little can be said about these effects from the point of view of small members alone. Scitovsky ventured an opinion that "if economic union should lead to a reallocation of current output from high- to low-cost firms either between or within national economies, such reallocation would probably be followed by a reallocation also of investment funds among the self-same firms."[9] In making new investments large firms have certain advantages; "the large firm usually has greater financial resources and easier access to capital than the small firm,"[1] and the large firm can engage in more scientific research and

---

7. *Ibid.,* p. 110.
8. *Ibid.,* chaps. i and iii.
9. *Ibid.,* p. 45.
1. *Ibid.,* p. 118; Rothschild, "The Small Nation and World Trade" and "Kleinstaat und Integration," stressed the importance of this factor, as did Marcy, *Economic Consequences,* pp. 276–277.

innovation. Scitovsky believed that private investors would only fully exploit the union-wide opportunities if there were long-run guarantees of free trade and unchanged exchange rates. The allocation between countries would change more if there were intra-union mobility of labor as well as capital as in a common market. Scitovsky reached the conclusion for Europe that "units that exploit economies of scale and location not available without economic union are almost certain to become monopolies or near-monopolies on an all-European scale. . . . International control of this type may be expected to assure an equitable distribution of the benefits of these investments between producers and users. . . . the main economies are said to be those of scale and not of location, and can therefore be realized more or less anywhere." [2]

More attention is now being paid to these location factors which Scitovsky brushed aside, or more broadly, to the whole category of external economies of scale. One difficulty in dealing with external economies of scale lies in the plethora of definitions of the concept. Since it was formulated by Alfred Marshall, the theory of decreasing costs arising from external economies has ranged the whole gamut from strict partial equilibrium assumptions to general equilibrium analysis. It has usually been conceived in a static framework, but from its inception it has been infused with an element of growth over time. Recently growth theorists have reformulated the concept for their own use. Broadly speaking, they regard as an external economy any cost reduction accruing to a firm, or any increase in demand for the industry's product, which results from an increased production in another firm or sector and which permits the utilization of lower cost capacity in the relevant firm.[3]

Many growth theorists have emphatically stated their belief that external economies in the sense of complementarities in production and consumption are much more important in developing countries than in large developed countries.[4] The smallness of markets in these countries limits the range of industrial activities, prevents the establishment of some industries requiring a large scale of production, and is likely to lead to monopolistic conditions in other product markets. Continued industrial development in these countries or the extension of

---

2. *Economic Theory*, p. 51.
3. The first and best-known attempt to define external economies from a growth viewpoint was that of Tibor Scitovsky, "Two Concepts of External Economies," *Journal of Political Economy*, LXI (April, 1954), 143–151.
4. *Ibid.*, p. 150; H. W. Arndt, "External Economies in Economic Growth," *Economic Record*, XXXI (Nov., 1955), 202; Marcus Fleming, "External Economies and the Doctrine of Balanced Growth," *Economic Journal*, LXV (June, 1955), 249.

national markets in the formation of customs unions and free trade areas are supposed to lead to decreasing costs in many industries—or, as some would have it, to external economies. Since small developed countries share these same characteristics, it is not surprising to find the same contention that these external economies are more numerous in small developed countries than in large developed countries.[5]

Membership in any regional trade organization which enables members to import raw or semifinished or fixed capital inputs from other members duty-free would certainly lower the cost of production in many industries. To the extent that intra-union competition leads to cost reductions in decreasing-cost industries, as discussed before, there may be further external economies to other firms in the form of cheaper inputs. The larger the aggregate size of the union the larger these gains, too, are likely to be. These lower input costs will be available to all firms in all countries of a union, large or small, disregarding possible differentials in transport costs.

However, certain types of external economy because of location may not accrue to all members of a union or regional organization. Recent attention on external economies and their relevance to trade groups has been focused on external economies due to the geographical proximity of industrial or urban complexes. Alfred Marshall declared that the external economies of scale resulting from "the concentration of specialized industries in particular localities" were the "most important" group.[6] E. A. G. Robinson in 1931 made a useful distinction between "mobile" and "immobile" external economies.[7] He contended that one group of external economies are "mobile" in the sense that they will accrue to firms in all localities of a country. Some of these are internationally mobile; for example, improvements in machinery or organization. Such economies would accrue to all members of a regional trade group.

"Immobile" economies on the other hand depend on the aggregate volume of production "of a kind in a neighborhood."[8] Location theorists have paid much more attention to economies of this type than have economists.[9] They distinguish two groups of "agglomera-

---

5. For example, Balassa, *Theory of Economic Integration*, p. 156.
6. Marshall, *Principles of Economics* (8th ed.; London, 1920, reprinted, 1956), pp. 264, 221.
7. E. A. G. Robinson, *The Structure of the Competitive Economy* (New York and London, 1931), pp. 142-143.
8. *Ibid.*
9. The use by location theorists of "agglomeration" effects is conveniently summarized by Walter Isard, *Location and Space Economy* (New York, 1956), chap. viii.

tion" effects. One group is comprised of "urbanization economies of all firms for all industries at a single location, consequent upon the enlargement of the total economic size (population, income, output or wealth) of that location, for all industries taken together." [1] Especially important are economies which result from the "higher level of use of the general apparatus of an urban structure," such as transportation and public amenities. The second group consists of "localization economies for all firms in a single industry at a single location, consequent upon the enlargement of the total output of that industry at that location." [2] For example, there are the gains of access to a larger pool of skilled labor. There is an important group based on the interdependence of related industries; the fuller use of specialized and auxiliary industrial, professional, and repair facilities.

Allyn Young in 1928 drew attention to the gains from specialization in a large market in his famous dictum that "the progressive division and specialization of industries is an essential part of the process by which the increasing returns are realized." [3] This form of industrial interdependence renders the total production necessary to exploit fully the economies of scale very much larger than appears from economies in individual industries. Scitovsky succinctly stated the principle in relation to the size of countries: "An economy that is large enough to provide domestic market outlets for the output of at least one optimum-sized plant in all industries producing final products may still be sub-optimal if some of these plants need equipment, servicing or other intermediate products, but provide too small a market outlet for some of these." [4] Plants in small countries tend to be more diversified in range of products produced.[5] Gains from increased specialization *within* plants and industries when a customs union increases the size of the markets could be substantial.

The importance of location to a small nation joining a regional trade group will depend on the proportion of immobile potential external economies. Of course, urbanization economies are immobile. They will accrue to a greater extent to the larger centers of agglomera-

---

1. *Ibid.*, p. 172.
2. *Ibid.*
3. Allyn Young, "Increasing Returns and Economic Progress," *Economic Journal*, XXXVIII (Dec., 1928), 527–542.
4. *Economic Consequences*, p. 283; cf. Jewkes, in *ibid.*, pp. 100–102, and Fabricant, in *ibid.*, pp. 43–46. Balassa, *Theory of Economic Integration*, pp. 156–159, discusses the significance of specialization in larger markets and in customs unions.
5. Balassa, *Theory of Economic Integration*, pp. 136–138; *Economic Consequences*, p. xviii.

tion which presumably are located in the larger nations. Similarly, the small nations may be precluded from benefiting from some of the external economies of localization if these occur in the large industrial complexes of the large member nations. The primary determinants of the distribution of these external economies will be the proximity of member nations, the range and interdependence of their established industries, and the location of industrial plants within these nations.

A crucial factor in determining the significance of these agglomeration effects is the extent of factor mobility between members. If only a customs union or a free trade area is formed there should always be some exchange rate that will enable all countries to have approximately the desired level of employment and balance of payments stability while each member specializes in the commodities in which it has a comparative advantage.[6] This implies that any country with a comparative advantage in the agricultural or raw-material-producing sectors may have to import a greater proportion of its manufacturing goods and forego the development of some manufacturing industries. But if free movement of labor as well as capital is permitted, the dangers of all manufacturing industries subject to agglomeration effects migrating to the large industrial centers are increased.

In the fifties, some European economists, notably François Perroux, were concerned that the agglomerative tendencies in a European common market would accentuate the regional disparities, harming such regions as the west and south of France and much of Italy.[7] Balassa in his survey of the European evidence asserted that the "spread-effects" emanating from highly developed regions "can be relied upon to counteract the polarization tendencies in a union of developed economies and are likely to lead to a reduction of regional disparities, *on the average.*"[8] The next section notes the concern over these location factors in the case of the Australia-New Zealand free trade discussions, and Section V examines the same concern in many developing countries.

The significance of external economies in a union, like that of internal economies, can only be verified or refuted by empirical study. Only one statistical study of external economies within a union or proposed union of countries is known to this writer, and that is the endeavor by P. G. Elkan to estimate the significance of "agglomera-

---

6. Scitovsky, *Economic Theory*, pp. 40–42.
7. See references given by Balassa, *Theory of Economic Integration*, pp. 202–204.
8. *Ibid.*, p. 204.

tion" tendencies in the event of completely free trade on all commodities between Australia and New Zealand.[9] His conclusions, which are based solely on an aggregative study of the distribution of manufacturing output in the Australian states and Canadian provinces, are unfortunately subject to some major qualifications.[1] At the Lisbon conference it was concluded that the main advantage of a large economy may lie in the gains from the specialization between closely related industries rather than in the greater exhaustion of internal economies. Whereas the internal economies of scale appeared to participants to be exhausted by firms of quite moderate size, these "external" economies appeared to be a more or less continuous function of size. Small nations are at a disadvantage compared with the moderately large "50 million" nations, but these latter nations in turn also appeared to be at a disadvantage compared with a very large country such as the United States.[2] So they may be, but in the absence of empirical studies of the specific industries in countries actually involved or thinking of becoming involved in regional trade groups we cannot gauge the importance or unimportance of "polarization" tendencies.

IV

Predictions based on a theoretical examination *in vacuo* of the factors that might affect the outcome for any small country joining a customs union, which were outlined in the previous two sections, have been conflicting and uncertain. It is time to consider the specific features that relate to smaller or less developed members in actual or proposed customs unions or free trade areas and the experience to date of the small developed countries that are members of actual regional trade arrangements.

One of the important objectives of the Rome Treaty is to insure the harmonious development of the economies of member states by mitigating the backwardness of the less developed regions. The treaty contains a number of provisions relating to the use of the European Investment Bank and the European Social Fund for less developed regions. The EEC has lately undertaken a new experiment to develop more rapidly the Italian Mezzogiorno. A survey showed that the chief

---

9. "Estimating New Zealand's Manufacturing Output in a Common Market with Australia," New Zealand Institute of Economic Research, Technical Memorandum No. 8 (Wellington, 1965).
1. See F. W. Holmes, "Freer Trade with Australia," New Zealand Institute of Economic Research, Discussion Paper No. 10 (Wellington, 1966), pp. 24–31.
2. See Robinson, in *Economic Consequences,* pp. xiii-xxii, for a summary of the views of the conference.

difficulty in establishing more advanced processing industries in the area "lies in the absence of the whole intricate and coherent industrial environment which a new firm would find ready to hand in areas which have already developed." [3] The very interesting conclusion the survey reached is that it is possible to establish such a complex of subsidiary industries for one branch of industry alone, in this case the heavy and medium engineering industry. Ironically, this method, which is already benefiting the chosen provinces of Bari and Taranto, is called "industrial development poles"!

Bela Balassa has made a survey of production and exports in ninety-one manufacturing industries in the EEC, using data for several years since the creation of the EEC. His finding is that "the fears expressed in various member countries of the Common Market concerning the demise of particular industries have not been realized. There are no examples of declining manufacturing industries in any of the member countries, nor have they experienced a wave of bankruptcies . . . and there is little evidence of frictional unemployment." [4] This statement applies to Italy, the least industrialized of the members, as well as to all the other members. Balassa attributes this result to national product differentiation. Multilateral reductions in tariffs have led to an increasing exchange of differentiated products between countries, to intra-industry specialization rather than to interindustry specialization. Countries have specialized in a narrower range of products, obtaining economies of scale through the lengthening of production runs, without the decline of any industries and without substantial changes in their structures of production.

The experience of the smaller and less industrialized Scandinavian countries is more pertinent. The Scandinavian countries began negotiations for a customs union before the formation of either the EEC or EFTA. The arguments in favor of a Nordic customs union then were that it would allow a better division of labor, aid the exploitation of potential large-scale economies, and lead to a more competitive climate.[5] In 1957 a final report proposed a customs union between Denmark, Norway, and Sweden, with the eventual participation of Finland and Iceland.[6] Norway was most concerned about the adverse effects of the suggested union because of the fears of the Norwegian busi-

---

3. EEC *Bulletin* (Jan., 1966), pp. 5–9.
4. "Tariff Reductions and Trade in Manufacturing among the Industrial Countries," *American Economic Review*, LVI (June, 1966), 472.
5. Nils Lundgren, "Nordic Common Market," *EFTA Bulletin* (March and April, 1966), provides a survey of past and present proposals for a Nordic union.
6. *Nordic Economic Cooperation*, Report by the Nordic Economic Cooperation Committee (Copenhagen, 1958).

ness community of being overwhelmed by competition from the larger and more diversified Swedish industry. Norway used the opportunity to exclude certain products from the proposed union which was to cover only 80 per cent of intra-Nordic trade. In 1959 the members of the proposed union acceded to EFTA, and interest in a Nordic union lapsed. Proposals were revived at a meeting of the Nordic Council in February, 1966. Since industrial trade between possible members has been very largely freed under EFTA, the arguments in favor of a union are now based on obtaining a better balance of power within EFTA and more bargaining power with the EEC or other countries in trade negotiations. At this time the highly-protected and narrowly-based Finnish manufacturing industries are considered the most vulnerable. The timetable of the EFTA-Finland agreement of 1961 which gave Finland associate membership in EFTA recognized these difficulties in giving Finnish industries a somewhat longer transitional period of adjustment. Similar treatment could be afforded Finnish industry in a Nordic union.[7]

An EFTA survey of economic integration in Scandinavia noted that "intra-Scandinavian trade takes place within a framework of integration between the Scandinavian countries, to a degree unparalleled elsewhere in the world." [8] A common labor market has been in effect in the four Continental Scandinavian countries since 1954. Free trade within the EFTA region has not had the deleterious results on industry in Norway and Denmark that many expected. "The advanced quality-minded Swedish market has also proved to be a convenient test ground for new products from the other countries and, ironically, it seems that those home market industries in Norway and Denmark which most feared competition from Sweden have benefited most from the gradual abolition of tariffs between the Scandinavian countries." [9] As in the EEC, intra-industry specialization has developed rapidly, even though these industries have faced increasing competition from British and Swiss firms as well as those in the other Scandinavian countries. Despite the high degree of factor mobility already existing among these countries no special permanent protection is considered necessary for the smaller, less industrialized members.

In contemplating a "Canada-U.S. Free Trade Arrangement" the Canadian-American Committee emphasized the great size disparity of these two countries:

---

7. Lundgren, "Nordic Common Market."
8. EFTA, *EFTA Trade, 1959–64* (Geneva, 1966), chap. B5, p. 26.
9. *Ibid.*, p. 28.

> For U.S. production, free access to the Canadian market would generally add about 10% to the present size of its domestic market....
>
> For Canadian production, on the other hand, free access to the U.S. market would add about 1,000% to the present size of its domestic market....
>
> To be sure, some Canadian manufacturing industries, and a larger portion of its extractive industry, are already able to compete against U.S. production for the total North American market without extensive scaling-up or modernization. And some industries whose natural market area is limited by transportation costs (e.g., cement) may also be ready now for free trade. But for much Canadian secondary industry, free access to the U.S. market would bring a totally new competitive environment requiring a drastic restructuring of productive capacity. In shifting from producing few copies of many items to producing many copies of a few items, plants will often have to be completely re-equipped and perhaps rebuilt, a process requiring major capital commitments which, once made, could not be liquidated.
>
> The necessity to restructure much of Canadian secondary industry . . . suggests that the transitional period affecting Canadian tariffs should be longer than that governing the tariffs of the United States, whose industry generally would require very little adjustment to prepare for the new situation. . . .
>
> The prospects of a drastic, costly, and irreversible restructuring of Canadian industry means that the commodity coverage, once set, must be permanent.[1]

Yet, they recommended that reciprocal free trade apply to all commodities, with the exception only of certain agricultural products and close derivatives. For all other products, tariffs would be eliminated in five equal annual cuts of 20 per cent in the United States but in Canada ten equal cuts of 10 per cent would double the period of adjustment in that country. They also advocated adjustment assistance, as provided in the United States under the Trade Expansion Act of 1962, for Canadian industries to develop their exports as well as to cushion the impact on domestic markets, a Canada-United States Investment Bank to facilitate adjustment to continental operation, and the possibility of temporarily maintaining government aids for certain geographic areas.

The 1965 New Zealand-Australia Free Trade Agreement provides only for limited free trade, after a transitional period of eight years, in some 60 per cent of the value of trade between the two countries,

---

1. Canadian-American Committee, *A Canada-U.S. Free Trade Arrangement* (Washington, D.C., and Montreal, 1963), pp. 75–76.

most of which was duty-free before the agreement.[2] In addition, there are a number of safeguards intended to prevent any undue disruption of industrial production. The agreement provides that either country may suspend its obligations, unilaterally if necessary, in respect to any products which are being imported "in such quantities and under such conditions as to cause or threaten serious injury to its producers of like or directly competitive products."[3] Other provisions relate to the deflection of trade resulting from unequal advantage in access to inputs of raw materials or fixed capital goods and from problems due to dumped and subsidized imports. A more unusual clause provides for the suspension or even the withdrawal of obligations for the products of any industry not at present planned or foreseen but later considered by one country to contribute to its economic development. Although there is provision for expansion of the commodities covered, the agreement in effect, by explicitly excluding "those goods the inclusion of which would be seriously detrimental to an industry in the territory of either Member State, or would be contrary to the national interest of either Member State," permits each country to continue the development of its manufacturing industries as it pleases. This provision was included deliberately to protect the many New Zealand industries in particular which have reached a less advanced stage than their Australian counterparts. It may in part, too, reflect a fear that "with differing levels of industrial development there would be a tendency for future industrial development to be concentrated in the larger and more industrialized country."[4]

One New Zealand economist has stressed the "polarization" argument.[5] In lieu of a free trade area he has proposed a "customs-drawback union" which is intended to insure that trade between members is competitive rather than complementary in the special sense that each country would export to the other an approximately equal value

---

2. For a history of the co-operation and the lack of co-operation between these two countries, including the 1965 agreement, see F. W. Holmes, "Freer Trade with Australia."

3. "New Zealand-Australia Free Trade Agreement," New Zealand House of Representatives, Parliamentary Paper A17 (1965), Article 9.

4. "New Zealand-Australia Free Trade Agreement," Canterbury Chamber of Commerce Bulletin No. 495 (June, 1966), p. 3. The significance of this quotation is that it is made by the Department of Industries and Commerce, the official New Zealand representative in the negotiations.

5. P. G. Elkan, in "How to Beat Backwash: The Case for Customs Drawback Unions," *Economic Journal*, LXXV (March, 1965), 44–60, "Estimating New Zealand's Manufacturing Output," and "Freer Trade with Australia: Why and How," New Zealand Institute of Economic Research, Discussion Paper No. 8 (Wellington, 1965).

of products in certain broad categories. At the same time members would benefit from the increased competition and greater economies of scale in a larger market. Apart from its cumbersome character and the questionable desirability of this type of balanced bilateral trade for commodity groups,[6] the conditional nature of its tariff concessions would seem to increase rather than reduce the degree of uncertainty in trade and therefore to frustrate the intention of giving members access to a larger market in these products. Moreover, it is very doubtful, especially for low-tariff products, that the degree of price elasticity of supply in these countries would overcome the attractions of the larger Australian market if these are as powerful as Elkan believes them to be.

The New Zealand insistence on excluding any tariff concessions on sensitive manufacturing products liable to be affected adversely by free trade is the most timid approach of all. It is explicable probably not so much by the size disparity of the two countries—which is only four to one—as by the virtually complete protection of New Zealand industries which have been under import licensing almost continuously since 1938. Additional safeguards such as a delayed introduction of free trade for the smaller and more vulnerable partner—as was built into the EFTA-Finland agreement and the 1963 Greece-EEC agreement and proposed for the Canada-U.S. Free Trade Arrangement—and provisions for adjustment assistance—as in the latter proposal—could have overcome most of the problems. Perhaps most regrettable is the fact that the manufacturing industries of both countries have foregone access to a nearby market which could have been used to test the exports of manufacturing products each country is seeking to develop at present in order to diversify its exports. The Scandinavian countries have recently found the markets of the neighboring members of EFTA valuable for this purpose.[7]

V

Since about 1960 there has been a veritable flood of published materials on the pros and cons of customs unions or free trade areas for developing countries. My purpose here is merely to draw parallels between the concerns of these writers and those who have considered the problems of small developed countries. I shall confine most of my

---

6. Cf. Balassa's objections to Latin American ideas of reciprocity (*Economic Development and Integration*, pp. 120–122).

7. *EFTA Trade, 1959–64*, chap. B5.

references to a few more important surveys of developing countries and regional trade prospects.[8] While it is true that "much has been said about economic integration in underdeveloped areas, but, so far, little has been accomplished,"[9] the importance of the possible access to larger markets for the large number of developing countries is obvious.

Several authors have asserted that the static gains from trade creation resulting from unions of developing countries are likely to be small and losses due to trade diversion may be greater than in the case of unions of developed countries.[1] This difference exists because the intra-area trade before union is small, the amount of overlapping in products produced is small, and in many cases the cheapest sources of supply lie outside the unions. Charles E. Staley disputes this contention for the Central American union.[2] Balassa adds that the existence of high tariffs, quotas, and overvalued exchange rates as in Latin America has led to the parallel development of some manufacturing industries in several developing countries and asserts that this offers scope for a "considerable degree of trade creation *and* diversion in this area."[3]

All these writers are emphatic, however, that the dynamic and long-run effects of regional trade groups of developing countries are certain to be of more importance than the static effects. One distinctive feature of the discussion concerning developing countries is the much lower importance attached to improvements in efficiency brought on by increased competition. R. L. Allen says typically that "in general these manufacturing industries, under present proposals, are not ex-

---

8. R. F. Mikesell, "The Theory of Common Markets as Applied to Regional Arrangements among Developing Countries," in *International Trade Theory in a Developing World*, ed. Roy Harrod and D. C. Hague (London, 1963); R. L. Allen, "Integration in Less Developed Areas," *Kyklos*, Fasc. 3 (1961), pp. 315–334; R. S. Bhambri, "Customs Unions and Underdeveloped Countries," *Economia Internazionale* (May, 1962); A. J. Brown, "Economic Separatism Versus a Common Market in Developing Countries," *Yorkshire Bulletin*, XIII (May, 1961), pp. 33–40, and (Nov., 1961), pp. 88–96; Sydney Dell, *Trade Blocs*, chaps. vi–vii. On Latin American unions there are several useful surveys: Victor L. Urquidi, *Free Trade and Economic Integration in Latin America* (Berkeley, 1962); Charles E. Staley, "Central American Integration," *Southern Economic Journal*, XXIX (Oct., 1962), pp. 88–95. The most thorough survey of the whole area is that by Bela Balassa, *Economic Development and Integration*.

9. Bela Balassa, *Trade Prospects for Developing Countries* (Homewood, Ill., 1964), p. 120.

1. Allen, "Integration in Less Developed Areas," pp. 330–332; Bhambri, "Customs Unions," pp. 236–238; Brown, "Economic Separatism," pp. 34–35. Cf. Viner, *The Customs Union Issue*, p. 135.

2. "Central American Integration."

3. *Economic Development and Integration*, p. 34; also *Theory of Economic Integration*, pp. 53–55.

posed to competition of any significance, since there are no counterpart industries in the other countries of the area."[4] A more basic point is raised by R. F. Mikesell: "Competition is by no means a popular principle in developing countries, and in Latin America regional trading arrangements are viewed more as mechanisms for development planning on a regional basis than as providing the basis for intra-regional competition."[5] Sydney Dell is even more emphatic: "To argue that the main aim should be to increase the competitiveness of existing Asian industry is to misunderstand the whole character and dimensions of the problem."[6] Moreover, if there are no alternative employment opportunities for resources so displaced, competition, he insists, will be detrimental to the total output of the union.

The essential point is that developing countries are almost wholly concerned with regional trade groupings as a means of affecting the future pattern of investment and productive capacity rather than as a means of attaining a more efficient utilization of inputs or even a greater utilization of existing capacity in present plants. They look upon these groupings as another instrument of policy to use in pursuit of the goal of economic growth. Rates of growth of export earnings that are regarded as unsatisfactory coupled with a desire to accelerate the rate of economic growth have led the countries of Asia and Latin America in particular toward import substitution and industrialization behind high walls of protection. With small oligopolistic domestic markets, sub-optimal plant or sub-optimal use of the most efficient plant will prevail in decreasing cost industries. Costs of protection are often great, and substitution for more capital-intensive durable products requiring a larger scale of production becomes more difficult and costly. These countries look upon customs unions or free trade areas as "a policy of regionally co-ordinated import substitution."[7] Regional free trade will provide needed access to larger markets for key capital goods and other large-scale industries. Much attention has also been

---

4. "Integration in Less Developed Areas," p. 330.
5. "The Theory of Common Markets," p. 218.
6. *Trade Blocs*, p. 216; Balassa objects to this reasoning (*Economic Development and Integration*, p. 105).
7. Economic Commission for Asia and the Far East (ECAFE), *Economic Bulletin for Asia and the Far East* (Dec., 1963), p. 95. Perhaps the best discussions of these ideas are to be found in this bulletin, pp. 94–96, and Balassa, *Economic Development and Integration*, chap. iii. Urquidi, *Free Trade*, documents Latin American views on this subject.

The regional commissions of the United Nations, especially those of Latin America and Asia, have played an important part in the development and spread of these ideas of regional trade and development. Raul Prebisch's report to the 1964 United Nations Conference on Trade and Development, *Towards a New Trade Policy for Development* (New York, 1964), made similar recommendations.

paid to the possibilities of greater specialization within industries and external economies of scale for the whole region when many complementary industries are developed simultaneously in member countries. "In short, the regional approach is, in the absence of a well-functioning multilateral trading system, the most promising way in which the economic growth of the developing countries can be accelerated without detriment to the efficiency and advantages of international specialization." [8]

In the Central American Common Market this principle of "planned complementarity" has been formally incorporated in the treaty. It provides for the joint planning and certification by all five members of "integration industries" for which the minimum capacity of a plant is considered to require access to the whole market. Each country is to receive one of these industries before any country has two. In LAFTA there is no formal provision for the certification of industries but the treaty stated the idea of complementarity agreements and several have been established. Some Western economists have raised doubts about the allocation of new investments by political negotiations between members, the chances of achieving the necessary coordination of development plans, and the dangers of monopoly.[9]

As in the case of small developed countries, some advocates of regional free trade for developing countries also anticipate gains from improved terms of trade, increased bargaining power in international negotiations, and increased investment, including investment from abroad. But these gains are usually regarded as of secondary importance by comparison with those due to economies of scale and complementarity.

The most striking feature of the writings on regional trade and developing countries is the pervading worry over "polarization" and "backwash" which will adversely affect the less industrialized members.[1] This concern no doubt reflects in part the views of Gunnar Myrdal and Raul Prebisch, who propounded these concepts with the developing countries and their low level of industrial development in mind. It is claimed that the experience of East Africa and of the former Federation of Rhodesia and Nyasaland vindicates these fears.[2] Many

---

8. ECAFE, *Economic Bulletin*, p. 95.
9. Allen, "Integration in Less Developed Areas," p. 325; Mikesell, "The Theory of Common Markets," p. 220; Elkan, "Freer Trade with Australia," p. 17. Cf. ECAFE, *Economic Bulletin*, p. 95.
1. Every one of the references in n. 8, p. 118, has a discussion of this topic. See in particular, Dell, *Trade Blocs*, chap. vi; Balassa, *Economic Development and Integration*, pp. 122–125; A. J. Brown, "Economic Separatism," Part II.
2. Dell, *Trade Blocs*, pp. 236–241, and Balassa, *Economic Development and Integration*, p. 125.

stress the unequal size of members of present and proposed free trade areas.³ Yet most authors appear to believe that such measures as the co-ordination of regional policies, longer transitional periods for the less developed members, and investment banks can overcome these dangers.⁴ A special chapter of the Montevideo Treaty contains a number of ways, including provision for the less advanced members to proceed more slowly with import liberalization, by which the economic growth of less advanced members may be stimulated. The Central American Common Market has provision for "integrated industries" in each country and an Integration Bank specifically charged with seeking a balanced economic development of member countries.

Hence, the general areas of concern in developing countries are much the same as those which have troubled the small developed countries. Both groups of countries have been fundamentally most concerned over opportunities and problems that arise because of economies of scale, internal and external. However, the relative emphasis has been somewhat different. The preoccupation of economists in developing countries with "planned complementarity," the playing down of the gains from competition, and greater worry over "polarization" than has been evident in the small developed countries are probably all explicable in large part by the great majority of developing countries' being considerably smaller in terms of national product than our group of small developed countries. Excluding Japan, India was the only developing country in 1964 which had a gross domestic product in excess of $20 billion, the upper limit for our small countries. A majority of the developing countries in Latin America and Africa had national products of less than $1 billion.⁵ Yet, the differences between small developed countries and developing countries are a question of degree only. The gross domestic product and industrial development of some large developing countries such as Brazil, India, Mexico, and Argentina are comparable with most of our small developed countries. This author rejects the idea sometimes put forward⁶ that we must construct a separate theory of customs unions for developing countries. Proponents of this course apparently believe, mistakenly

---

3. Balassa, *Economic Development and Integration*, p. 125; Allen, "Integration in Less Developed Areas," p. 321; Staley, "Central American Economic Integration," p. 90; Dell, *Trade Blocs*, p. 230.
4. Dell, *Trade Blocs*, p. 257; Balassa, *Economic Development and Integration*, p. 125; Bhambri, "Customs Unions," pp. 246–252, and references therein.
5. United Nations, *Yearbook of National Accounts Statistics*, 1964, Table 9B.
6. Dell, *Trade Blocs*, chap. vii; Demas, *Economics of Development in Small Countries*, p. 86; B. F. Massell and C. A. Cooper, "Toward a General Theory of Customs Unions for Developing Countries," *Journal of Political Economy*, LXXIII (Oct., 1965), 461–476.

in my view, that such a theory would be equally applicable to all developing countries but not applicable to any developed countries.

VI

In conclusion, country size can only be related indirectly to the outcome of joining a customs union or free trade area. There is no simple connection between economies of scale, internal or external, and the size of country in terms of its national output. For example, the proximate causes of the short-run reallocation of existing capacities are the unit costs of production and the amounts of unutilized capacities in all plants. The ultimate causes include the following: whether costs decrease continuously or not, the extent of competitiveness between the pre-union ranges of production of such products in the small country and in other members, the degree of competition in the relevent industries in the small country and in other members before and after the union, and product differentiation. Similarly, many factors decide the effect of joining a union on the allocation of new investment expenditures and the location of industries. The effects on real incomes of small countries which we have not considered explicitly are even more complex than these effects on individual industries.

As in several other contexts considered in this book, no generalizations concerning small nations and customs unions or free trade areas seem possible. The circumstances of each small nation must be investigated, but regrettably the empirical side of the issues has been neglected and has yet to give conclusive evidence of the gains and losses of small nations in competition with larger neighbors. What evidence there is for the less industrialized regions of Italy and France in the EEC and Norway and Denmark in EFTA suggests that pre-union fears for smaller member countries in regional trade arrangements have been unduly pessimistic.

CHAPTER VIII

Summary and Conclusions

In Chapter I it was decided that national income could be employed as the index of national size in the subsequent models. The national income measure is appropriate in the analysis of diseconomies of small-scale production in small countries, the derivative arguments concerning dependence in these countries, and the dangers to them of joining a customs union or free trade area. In the Graham model of comparative advantage the measure of national size is that of productive capacity, but in most cases national income should provide a close approximation. Similarly, the arguments relating to small countries and their foreign trade multipliers or the devaluation of their currencies are also related to countries small in terms of national income.

There is an interesting parallel in the way in which the variable of country size has been formally introduced into three models. Both Guy Orcutt in the context of his discussion of "Exchange Rate Adjustment and the Relative Size of the Depreciating Bloc" and Jan Tinbergen in his model of "Customs Unions: Influence of Their Size on Their Effect" employed the device of starting with a given number of identical "country" units and introduced the size of countries by hypothetically varying the number of these units which comprise the countries in their models. I used the same technique when analyzing the possible relationships between country size and foreign trade multipliers in the Appendix to Chapter IV.

In these models and in Graham's model of comparative advantage, country size is introduced directly as a variable. Similarly, in the arguments concerning economies of scale in decreasing-cost industries and the effect on a small country of joining a customs union or free trade area, the connection between country size and economies of scale is through the total value of goods and services produced.

However, in other arguments small countries have been supposed to behave similarly under certain circumstances, not directly because they are small, but because, being small, they supposedly have certain trade characteristics in common which lead to the predicted results. For example, the supposed high ratio of international trade flows to national product in smaller countries has been held to make these countries more unstable and to lower the value of their foreign trade multipliers, other things being equal. A high degree of commodity and geographic concentration of exports is also supposed to accentuate the instability of these countries.

These claims led me to test, by multiple regression analyses, the importance of country size (gross domestic product) as a determinant of two features of international trade, namely, the ratio of international trade to national product and the degree of commodity concentration of export trade. The results of these empirical tests were startling; size of country was not a major determinant of the trade ratios of some sixty countries in 1964 and it was not even a significant factor in the determination of commodity concentration of exports. Moreover, all the six variables tested in each regression accounted for less than one half the total intercountry variation of these two features. What influence the size of a country has on the trade ratios in particular is in actuality swamped by that on the many other important factors affecting international trade flows. It was found that small countries do not generally have the trade characteristics which the builders of the models believed them to have. If a small country is defined as any country whose GDP was less than $20 billion in 1964, it is quite clear that the trade ratios and degrees of export concentration of these countries vary widely around the all-country averages.

Furthermore, many of the countries which have relatively high trade ratios have exceptionally low commodity concentration in their exports and vice versa. Thus a collection of models such as those in this study—which concern countries having high trade ratios and high degrees of commodity concentration in their export trade, a small share of world markets for their major exports, and other characteristics—cannot apply to a single group of countries. One certainly cannot apply the models discussed here consistently to all small countries, as I had originally sought. Yet, I still found it very worthwhile to examine the nature and merits of the various arguments numerous authors have put forward concerning small countries and to consider to what extent they apply to a more homogeneous group of fifteen small developed countries.

In most cases these models were not very helpful to understanding the international problems and experiences of these countries, for two reasons. First, even within this group, several of the countries did not

Summary and Conclusions   125

have one or more of the attributes that the models ascribed to small countries. Nine of the fifteen countries had trade ratios which were above the average for all sixty countries included in the regressions. Even here the association of high trade ratios with smallness is partly spurious for the European countries. However, only two of the countries had above average degrees of commodity concentration in their export trade. Similarly, few, if any, occupy such a small share of the foreign markets for their major exports that they can be regarded as price-takers. The second unsatisfactory aspect of the arguments or models is that they omit many factors which are clearly too important to be omitted. For example, in predicting the possible effect that membership in a customs union may have on the production of decreasing cost industries in a small country, one must consider, among other things, the amount of product differentiation, the economies of scale in the industries actually produced by the small country before union, and the degree of competition prevailing in these industries in the country before and after union. The connection between size of nations and each of these factors is tenuous.

For these two reasons some of the generalizations concerning small countries must be rejected completely. The very common argument that devaluation by a small country will be effective because the small share of its exports in world markets will mean a high foreign elasticity of demand for its exports is clearly fallacious. The belief that the export receipts of small countries will be more unstable than those of most countries is invalidated by the statistics of Coppock's comprehensive study. During the period 1946–1958 only two of the fifteen countries—Finland and Australia—had more than the average amount of instability for all the eighty-three countries Coppock studied. Switzerland and Ireland were actually the two most stable countries. Concerning other arguments, such as those which predict the elimination of most of the manufacturing industries of small countries joining a regional trade grouping which contains larger countries, what evidence there is does not support the contentions of previous writers.

On the other hand, some of the models help in explaining aspects of the behavior of some small countries. Graham's multi-country, multi-good model produces some valuable suggestions concerning the international trade of small nations. It indicates a tendency for most small nations to enjoy greater gains from trade, coupled with a susceptibility to rather large changes in their terms of trade and real incomes when the world demand or supply conditions for their traded commodities do change. However, as noted in Chapter II, the influence of the size of countries on the actual patterns of international trade is often swamped by location, trade barriers, and other factors. The matrix multiplier can explain why some countries have experienced balance of payments difficulties in periods of high export receipts. It was also observed that capital formation in most small countries, including the industrialized European countries, is dependent on imports for more than one third, and in several cases more than one half, of investment goods. One could perhaps successfully relate the contemporary concern over the "trade gap" to the smallness of economies and their industrial structure.

One notable feature of the scattered literature on the international trade of small countries is the preponderance of pessimistic arguments. It has been repeatedly suggested that small countries will be particularly unstable and dependent in various senses, that income adjustments will easily overflow into balance of payments problems, and that membership in regional trade groupings may have dire consequences for the industries of small countries. Admittedly some counter advantages of smallness have been put forward, notably that devaluation will readily correct a balance of payments disequilibrium of a small country. It has also been suggested that small countries may be more adaptable to change because of their greater cultural homogeneity and that overseas borrowing can achieve a larger proportionate addition to domestic capital formation in a small country than in a large country. But these favorable arguments are infrequent compared with the pessimistic ones. Further, the ancient Classical argument that small (and poor) nations will enjoy greater gains from trade is seldom heard today.

This "size pessimism" is difficult to understand in view of the outstanding stability of export receipts in many small countries and the relatively high rates of economic growth which many of them have had, despite, in the cases of Austria, Finland, and Israel, unusual barriers to growth. One explanation may be that most of the small developed countries do have large foreign trade sectors in relation to the aggregate sizes of their economies and may therefore be more aware of actual and possible disturbances in this sector, even though the historical experience of most of these countries in the postwar period gives no cause for their being more concerned over international trade difficulties than other countries.

Another thread of thought woven through this study is the close parallel between many theories and arguments concerning the trade difficulties of small developed countries and the ideas and theories relating to developing countries. This parallel is evident in the arguments about the instability of export receipts and dependence on imports. It is most remarkable in the recent literature on regional trade and customs unions. Both developing countries and small developed countries have been concerned over the smallness of their domestic markets, their high unit costs of production, the possible short-run dangers of facing competition with larger neighbors in a regional trade area, and the long-run danger of polarization of industries in large member countries. This parallelism is no doubt largely explained by the fact that both small developed countries and developing countries are small in the relevant sense of having small aggregate markets for the products of decreasing cost manufacturing industries, relative to those of the more industrialized neighbors in their regions. Chapter VII, however, indicates that there may be mitigating factors and the outcome of a union of countries will not be easy to predict.

This study has attempted to collate and assess diverse aspects of the international trade of small nations. Their smallness does play a limited role in explaining international trade problems of some countries. The primary conclusion of this study, however, is that small countries are a heterogeneous group which do not have uniform trade characteristics and cannot be expected to behave in the same way under similar circumstances. Furthermore, it was found in Chapter II that country size together with several other variables cannot explain more than a small part of the total intercountry variation of international trade ratios or the degree of commodity concentration of exports. This has important consequences. A "general" theory of international trade relating to broad groups of countries which is based on the assumption that the trade of these nations share certain features will have a very limited application.

Rather than attempt to develop general theories which will relate to all small or all developing countries, or any other such preselected group of countries, one should consider *for each model* only those countries which do have the characteristics or relationships upon which the model is based. The set of countries to which one may apply, for example, a model of devaluation in which the devaluing country is assumed to have no perceptible influence on the foreign markets for its exports and to have a high trade ratio is likely to be different from the set to which one may apply a foreign trade multiplier model where countries have a high marginal propensity to import and insignificant foreign repercussions. Sound predictive models can be constructed only with particular countries in mind, and the results of these models cannot be extended to other countries which, upon inspection, do not share the same characteristics.

Appendix I

Analysis of Trade Ratios, 1963–1964

Country	X + M/GDP	GDP ($U.S. millions)	GDP per capita ($U.S.)	Percentage GDP produced by industry	Population mid-1964 (millions)	Total area (000 hectares)	Fixed capital formation (percentage of GDP)
AFRICA							
Congo, Dem. Rep. of	60	1,111	73	31	15.3	234.5	14
Mauritius	102	156	216	19	0.7	0.2	19
Morocco	44	1,983	153	23	13.0	44.4	11
South Africa	52	13,728	700	40	17.5	122.3	20
Sudan	47	859	67	6	12.8	250.6	17
Tanzania	60	817	82	7	10.0	93.7	12
Togo	43	86	55	10	1.6	5.7	8
Tunisia	52	955	209	18	4.6	12.5	25
NORTH AMERICA							
Canada	43	40,577	2,106	34	19.2	997.6	23
United States	9	576,758	3,002	34	192.1	936.3	15
LATIN AMERICA							
Barbados	125	90	371	9	0.2	.0	21
Bolivia	45	526	144	27	3.7	109.9	15
Chile	23	3,872	456	26	8.5	74.2	14
Colombia	25	4,537	268	22	15.1	113.8	17
Costa Rica	53	374	270	14	1.4	5.1	14
Ecuador	36	949	194	21	4.9	27.7	17
El Salvador	41	485	178	18	2.7	2.1	11
Guatemala	33	1,262	295	16	4.3	10.9	13
Honduras	46	394	195	15	2.1	11.2	13
Jamaica	81	912	528	26	1.7	1.1	19
Mexico	21	16,967	428	31	39.6	197.3	16
Nicaragua	62	365	229	17	1.6	14.8	17
Panama	76	572	483	19	1.2	7.6	15
Paraguay	33	241	126	17	1.9	40.7	15
Peru	51	2,707	240	27	11.4	128.5	25

Appendix I (cont.)

Country	X + M/GDP	GDP ($U.S. millions)	GDP per capita ($U.S.)	Percentage GDP produced by industry	Population mid-1964 (millions)	Total area (000 hectares)	Fixed capital formation (percentage of GDP)
Puerto Rico	112	2,489	963	26	2.6	0.9	26
Trinidad and Tobago	148	586	617	46	0.9	0.5	29
Uruguay	26	1,479	558	46	2.7	18.7	13
Venezuela	58	6,673	792	40	8.4	91.2	20
ASIA							
Burma	31	1,894	80	17	23.7	67.8	16
Cambodia	38	651	111	12	5.7	18.1	17
Ceylon	56	1,561	142	7	11.0	6.5	14
Iran	35	3,913	176	30	22.9	164.8	13
Iraq	83	1,298	175	47	7.0	44.9	15
Israel	67	2,685	1,084	27	2.5	2.1	31
Japan	22	69,555	718	32	96.9	37.0	34
Jordan	60	372	204	10	1.8	9.7	13
Korea, Rep. of	22	3,961	143	13	27.6	9.8	11
Malaya	89	1,796	236	18	7.8	13.1	18
Philippines	41	4,027	129	22	31.3	30.0	15
Taiwan	36	1,498	122	25	12.1	3.6	14
Thailand	36	3,273	113	14	28.8	51.4	21
Vietnam, Rep. of	27	1,166	74	13	15.7	17.1	8
EUROPE							
Austria	52	7,456	1,033	42	7.2	8.4	24
Belgium-Luxembourg	77	14,277	1,472	36	9.7	3.4	21
Cyprus	66	347	591	21	0.6	0.9	13
Denmark	64	7,950	1,684	31	4.7	4.3	22
France	28	76,460	1,579	40	48.4	54.7	21
Finland	44	4,228	923	29	4.6	33.7	25
Greece	31	3,833	450	21	8.5	13.2	22
Ireland	70	2,550	895	32	2.8	7.0	19

Appendix I (cont.)

Country	X + M/GDP	GDP ($U.S. millions)	GDP per capita ($U.S.)	Percentage GDP produced by industry	Population mid-1964 (millions)	Total area (000 hectares)	Fixed capital formation (percentage of GDP)
Italy	34	52,731	1,032	36	51.0	30.1	21
Malta	123	126	388	27	.3	.03	21
Netherlands	94	17,350	1,431	41	12.1	3.4	25
Norway	84	6,951	1,882	30	3.7	32.4	29
Portugal	54	3,803	418	44	9.1	8.9	17
Spain	26	17,091	545	30	31.3	50.5	24
United Kingdom	40	92,071	1,698	41	54.2	24.4	17
West Germany	38	99,059	1,766	45	56.1	24.7	26
AUSTRALIA	34	20,122	1,807	33	11.1	769.5	26
Mean—60 countries	54	11,776	618	26	16.8	85.0	18

Sources: Cols. (1), (2), (3), (4), and (7): United Nations, *Yearbook of National Accounts Statistics*, 1965, Tables 9B and 3, for 1963–1964. Col. (5): For most countries, *UN Monthly Bulletin of Statistics*. For a few countries Col. (5) derived from (2) / (3). Col. (6): *FAO Production Yearbook*, 1964. Statistics for Israel and Cambodia in Cols. (2) and (3) converted into U.S. dollars at nominal exchange rates rather than purchasing power parity rates as used for other countries. South African statistics include those of Basutoland, South-West Africa, and Bechuanaland.

Appendix II

Analysis of Commodity Concentration of Exports, 1963–1964

Country	Hirschman Indices of commodity concentration of exports	Area (000 hectares)	Population mid-1964 (millions)	GDP ($U.S. millions)	GDP per capita ($U.S.)	Percentage GDP produced by industry	Value of exports ($U.S. millions)
AFRICA							
Congo, Dem. Rep. of	45.61	234.5	15.0	1,111	73	31	318
Kenya	38.03	58.3	9.1	861	95	11	150
Libya	99.17	176.0	1.6	311	199	20	709
Malawi	48.48	11.9	3.0	147	49	7	28
Mauritius	98.34	.2	.7	156	216	19	77
South Africa	19.14	122.3	17.5	13,728	700	40	1,456
Sudan	56.28	250.6	12.8	859	67	6	198
Tanzania	73.00	93.7	10.0	817	82	7	208
Togo	49.13	5.7	1.6	86	55	10	30
Tunisia	23.80	12.5	4.6	955	209	18	127
Uganda	60.96	24.0	7.3	576	78	11	186
Zambia	90.84	74.6	3.6	949	264	58	441
NORTH AMERICA							
Canada	18.27	997.6	19.2	40,577	2,106	34	7,681
United States	0.99	936.3	192.1	576,758	3,002	34	26,229
LATIN AMERICA							
Argentina	29.74	277.9	22.0	13,476	612	36	1,410
Barbados	82.44	.0	.2	90	371	9	36
Brazil	54.10	851.2	78.8	11,925	156	26	1,430
Chile	67.52	74.2	8.0	3,666	446	26	532
Colombia	73.29	113.8	15.4	4,537	268	22	548
Costa Rica	49.62	5.1	1.4	374	270	14	114
Ecuador	59.75	27.7	4.9	949	194	21	156
El Salvador	56.27	2.1	2.7	485	178	18	178
Honduras	43.40	11.2	2.1	394	195	15	95
Jamaica	52.91	1.1	1.7	912	528	26	221

Appendix II (cont.)

Country	Hirschman Indices of commodity concentration of exports	Area (000 hectares)	Population mid-1964 (millions)	GDP ($U.S. millions)	GDP per capita ($U.S.)	Percentage GDP produced by industry	Value of exports ($U.S. millions)
Mexico	21.38	197.3	39.6	16,967	428	31	1,036
Nicaragua	46.71	14.8	1.6	335	217	17	100
Panama	57.38	7.6	1.2	572	483	19	68
Trinidad and Tobago	76.90	.5	.9	586	617	46	405
Venezuela	70.72	91.2	8.4	6,673	792	40	2,742
ASIA							
Burma	63.76	67.8	23.7	1,894	80	17	271
Ceylon	64.53	6.5	11.0	1,561	142	7	394
India	21.78	326.3	471.6	36,012	78	19	1,748
Iran	70.96	164.8	22.9	3,913	176	30	1,254
Israel	40.65	2.1	2.5	2,685	1,084	27	352
Japan	12.83	37.0	96.9	69,555	718	32	6,674
Jordan	46.08	9.7	1.8	372	204	10	26
Korea, Rep. of	18.53	9.8	27.6	3,961	143	13	119
Malaya	54.01	13.1	7.8	1,796	236	18	909
Pakistan	42.40	94.6	100.8	7,824	79	12	427
Philippines	35.43	30.0	31.3	4,027	129	22	743
Syria	52.15	18.4	5.4	759	152	13	176
Taiwan	31.94	3.6	12.1	1,498	122	25	434
Thailand	42.90	51.4	29.7	3,273	113	14	599
Vietnam, Rep. of	69.77	17.1	15.7	1,166	74	13	48
EUROPE							
Austria	10.81	8.4	7.2	7,456	1,033	42	1,446
Belgium-Luxembourg	11.37	3.4	9.7	14,277	1,472	36	5,590
Cyprus	37.08	.9	.6	347	591	21	58
Denmark	15.66	4.3	4.7	7,950	1,684	31	2,119
France	9.18	54.7	48.4	76,460	1,579	40	8,993
Finland	38.07	33.7	4.6	4,228	923	29	1,291

Appendix II (cont.)

Country	Hirschman Indices of commodity concentration of exports	Area (000 hectares)	Population mid-1964 (millions)	GDP ($U.S. millions)	GDP per capita ($U.S.)	Percentage GDP produced by industry	Value of exports ($U.S. millions)
Greece	42.48	13.2	8.5	3,833	450	21	309
Ireland	30.64	7.0	2.8	2,550	895	32	622
Italy	12.61	30.1	51.0	52,731	1,032	36	5,956
Malta	36.12	.03	.3	126	388	27	19
Netherlands	9.60	3.4	12.1	17,350	1,431	41	5,808
Norway	16.77	32.4	3.7	6,951	1,882	30	1,290
Portugal	14.89	8.9	9.1	3,803	418	44	516
Spain	24.73	50.5	31.3	17,091	545	30	954
Turkey	34.51	78.1	31.1	9,297	299	17	411
United Kingdom	13.54	24.4	54.2	92,071	1,698	41	12,357
West Germany	14.80	24.7	56.1	99,059	1,766	45	16,215
AUSTRALIA	36.69	769.5	11.1	20,122	1,807	33	3,044
Mean—62 countries	42.6	107.6	27.3	20,900	587	25	2,065

Sources: Col. (2): *FAO Production Yearbook*, 1964. Col. (3): For most countries, *UN Monthly Bulletin of Statistics*. For a few countries, Col. (3) obtained from (4) ÷ (5). Cols. (4), (5), and (6): United Nations, *Yearbook of National Accounts Statistics*, 1965. Tables 9B and 3, for 1963 and 1964. Cols. (1) and (7): United Nations, *Yearbook of International Trade Statistics*, 1964. Indices in Col. (1) calculated from data in country tables for the 4 largest 3-digit SITC commodities in each country. Some statistics in Cols. (1) and (5-7) refer to 1963. Value of exports of Iran taken from International Monetary Fund, *International Financial Statistics*.

Index

Absorption approach to devaluation, 82
Alejandro, Carlos, 80n
Alexander, Sydney, 74n
Allen, R. L., 118–119
Area, as criterion of nation size, 4–6
Argentina: balance of payments difficulties, 63; gross domestic product, 121
Australia, 31; agglomeration tendencies in free trade area, 112; borrowing overseas capital, 43; commodity-weighted share of world exports, 42, 78; gross domestic product, 33; instability (1946–58), 125; largest world supplier of its main export products, 78; New Zealand-Australia Free Trade Agreement, 115–117; pulp, paper, and wool products, 49; ratio of imports to domestic product, 54; staple exports, percentages, 41; susceptibility to balance of payments difficulties, 63; trade dependence, 40; trade with United Kingdom, 35
Austria, 32; commodity-weighted share of world exports, 42, 78; devaluation of currency, 71, 85; high growth rate, 43, 126

Balance of payments: effect of national size on, 53, 61–65; stability of, 53, 111
Balassa, Bela, 42n, 102n, 103, 110n, 111, 113, 117n, 118
Balogh, T., 75n
Bastable, C. F., 86–87
Belgium-Luxembourg: commodity-weighted share of world exports, 42; gross domestic product, 33; growth rate, 43; index of commodity concentration of exports, 34; proximity to major markets, 5; ratio of largest export market to gross domestic product, 47; stability of export receipts, 50; trade ratio, 30, 34
Bilateral trade, in Graham model, 86–88
Bloomfield, Arthur J., 63
Brazil: commodity concentration of exports, 29; gross domestic product, 33, 121
Bretton Woods Agreement (1944), 71
Bruno, M., 40n

Canada, growth rate, 43
Canada-U.S. Free Trade Arrangement, 114–115, 117
Canada-U.S. Investment Bank, 115
Capital formation: fixed, as percentage of gross domestic product, 38–39t, 128–130; dependence on imports, 37–40
Caves, Richard E., 89
Central American Common Market, 118, 120, 121; Integration Bank, 121
Chenery, Hollis B., 4, 31n, 37, 40n, 103–104
Chile, trade ratio, 30
Chipman, John S., 16, 56, 88n, 89n, 95n
Columbia, trade ratio, 30
Commodity concentration of exports, 11, 12, 14, 21–30, 124, 125, 127; and country

Index 135

size, 28t; in a Graham model, 92–93; and instability, 50t; measurement of, 26–27; table of, by country, 131–133
Commodity concentration of imports, 14
Commodity-weighted shares of world exports: and elasticity of demand for exports, 40, 78; measurement of, 40–42
Comparative advantage, 14, 16, 99, 111; *see also* Graham model of comparative advantage
Coppock, Joseph, 26n, 46, 47, 48, 49, 50, 51, 71, 125; indices of export instability, 50t
Country size, *see* Nation size
Customs drawback union, 116–117
Customs union: adverse effects on small nations in union with large country, 99–100; degree of product differentiation and, 99; for developing countries, 117–122; economies of scale and, 18–19, 96, 97, 101, 102–107 *(see also* Economies of scale) ; effects of aggregate size on, 97–98; effects on individual countries, 96, 98, 112–117; effects on production in decreasing-cost industries, 99–107; effects on small countries, 96–122; external economies, 109–112; importation of raw, semi-finished, and fixed capital, 109; investment possibilities, effects on, 107–108; lack of competition, effects of, 101, 104; location factors, 108, 109–111; static theory of, 92–99, 104, 118
Cyprus, trade ratio, 30

Decreasing cost industries: as determinant of international trade, 16–20; effect of trade liberalization on, 99–107, 108–109, 123, 125
Dell, Sidney, 119
Demas, William G., 4
Denmark: bacon and butter trade, 41; commodity-weighted share of world exports, 42; EEC, EFTA, and, 113–114; growth rate, 43; proximity to major markets, 5; and United Kingdom trade (dairy products) , 35
Dependence, *see* Trade dependence
Depression, effect on growth rates, 46
Deutsch, Karl, 23n
Devaluation, 13, 71, 123; primary effects, 72–81; secondary effects, 81–85
Developing countries: customs unions for, 117–122; similarities to small developed countries, 12, 36, 37, 42, 53, 65, 86, 92, 121–122, 126–127
Diseconomies of small-scale production: customs unions, as escape from, 101–107; in small nations, 7–9; and trade characteristics of small nations, 15–20

East Africa, 120
Eckstein, Alexander, 23n
Economies of scale, 3, 4, 7, 31n, 37, 42; and customs union, 99–107; as determinant of international trade, 16–20; external economies and customs unions, 108–112
Edwards, C. D., 9
Elasticities of demand: and devaluation, 72–81; and export shares, 40–42; in small countries, 75–78
Elasticities of substitution, in Graham model of comparative advantage, 88, 91
Elasticities of supply, and devaluation, 79–81
Elkan, P. G., 111–112, 116–117
England, exports as percentage of company output, 18
European Economic Community (EEC) : Balassa studies on, 113; development of Italian Mezzogiorno, 112–113, 122; expansion of trade in, 35, 106; exploitation of economies of scale, 103; and France, 122; and Greece, 117; New Zealand's concern with, 34; and Scandinavian countries, 113–114
European Free Trade Area (EFTA) , 34, 106; and Scandinavian countries, 113–114, 117, 122

European Investment Bank, 112
European Social Fund, 112
Exports: commodity concentration of, 14–35; geographic concentration of, 14, 21–22, 34–35

Fabricant, Solomon, 8
Finland, 31, 32; commodity-weighted shares of world exports, 42; devaluation, 71, 85; EFTA and, 117; growth rate high, 43, 126; instability (1946–58), 125; largest world supplier of its main export products, 78; newsprint and pulp exports, 41, 49; Nordic customs union and, 113; paper products, 49; wool products, 49
Fleming, Marcus, 80–81, 84–85
Foreign repercussions, 54, 56, 59–61, 82
Foreign trade multipliers, 11, 13, 29, 30, 51–52, 123, 124, 127; and balance of payments, 53–65; foreign repercussions, 55–56, 59–62, 63, 64, 65
France: ex-colonial and cultural ties, effect on markets, 35; import ratio, 54; south of, effect of EEC on, 111; veto of United Kingdom in EEC, 34
Free trade areas: effect on small countries, 96–97, 103, 111-117; *see also* Customs union, European Economic Community, European Free Trade Area, Latin American Free Trade Area

Geographic concentration of exports, 12, 14, 21–22, 34–35, 46–47; in small countries, 33t
Germany: depression, effect on, 46; Nazi Germany, exploitation of small mid-European suppliers, 48; *see also* West Germany
Graham, Frank, 7, 86–95
Graham model of comparative advantage, 20, 21–22, 125; measure of country size in, 11, 30, 89–90, 123; a small nation in, 20, 36, 86–95; specialization advantages shown, 36; *see also* Comparative advantage
Greece, EEC and, 117
Gross domestic product: as determinant of trade characteristics, 22–28; as measure of country size, 11; *see also* National income
Growth rates: of developing countries, 119; of small nations, 42–44, 44t

Hicks-neutral technological change, and immiserizing growth, 95
Hirschman, Albert O., 14–15, 21, 22, 48; indices of commodity concentration, 26, 28 (fig. 2), 32t, 34, 41, 48, 131–133t
Holmes, F. W., 116n

Iceland, 31; Nordic customs union, 113
Immiserizing growth, 95
Imperial preference, 34
Imports: geographical concentration, 14–15; import content of capital formation, 37
India, gross national product, 121
Indonesia, gross domestic product, 33
Industrialization, and trade ratios, 22–35
Industries: factors affecting costs, 105–106; *see also* Decreasing cost industries
Instability of export receipts, 46–52
Instability of national income, 11, 44–52, 50t, 126–127
International Economic Association, conference at Lisbon, 3, 5, 9–10, 12–13, 16, 18, 32, 42, 50, 103, 105, 112
Iran, trade ratio, 30
Ireland: borrowing overseas capital, 43; commodity-weighted share of world exports, 42; dependence on one market, 34; growth rate, 43; high export ratio

Index 137

and high geographic concentration, relation to gross domestic product, 47; stability of export receipts, 50, 125; trade ratio, 30, 34
Isard, Walter, 109n
Israel, 32, 40n, 43n; borrowing overseas capital, 43; devaluation of currency, 71, 85; high growth rate, 43, 126
Italy: effect of EEC on, 111, 112, 113; Mezzogiorno development, 112–113; stable and profitable exports, 18

Japan, 121

Kemp, Murray, 72, 84
Kindleberger, Charles P., 61, 63–64
Kuwait, 31
Kuznets, Simon, 6n, 12, 16, 21, 42–44

Latin American Free Trade Area (LAFTA), 97n, 103, 120
Leduc, G., 10, 42
Leontief coefficients, 36–37
Levin, Jonathan V., 53n
Lipsey, Robert E., 23n, 24
Lisbon conference, *see* International Economic Association
Lloyd, Peter J., 57n, 63, 64
Location, and international trade patterns, 6, 26, 35, 95, 126
Luxembourg, *see* Belgium-Luxembourg

MacGregor, D. H., 5
Machlup, Fritz, 55–56, 61, 66, 68
McKenzie, Lionel, 89, 89n, 91, 91n
Maizels, Alfred, 23n, 37n
Marcy, G., 10, 18, 105–106
Marginal propensity to import, 53–70, 82; in small nations, 54
Marginal propensity to spend, 53–70
Marsan, V. A., 18
Marshall, Alfred, 6, 15, 24, 86, 87, 108, 109
Matrix multipliers, 56-64, 66–70, 126
Meade, James, 16–17, 72, 84, 97
Metzler, Lloyd, 56, 62n, 67
Mexico, gross domestic product, 121
Michaely, Michael, 22, 41–42, 48, 78
Mikesell, R. F., 119
Mill, J. S., 87, 91
Monopolies, and commodity concentration of exports, 48n
Monopolistic competition, and trade in a customs union, 98–107
Montevideo Treaty, 121
Myrdal, Gunnar, 120

Narrow resource base, and pattern of international trade, 4–5, 15–21
Nation size: absence of empirical studies on, 96; and area, 4–6, 10; attention in literature, 3, 4; in bilaterial trade, 86–87, 88, 89; commodity concentration of exports and, 14–35, 28t; definition of, 4–13; foreign trade multiplier and, 53–70; geographic concentration of exports and, 21–22; growth rates, effect on, 42–44; national income and, *see* National income; population and, 9, 10, 12–13, 41; productive capacity and, 6–7; trade ratios and, 14–35, 25t
National income: as criterion of nation size, 7n, 7–9, 10, 11–12, 17n, 97, 123;

dependence on international trade, 36; instability of, 42–45; ratio of, to international trade, 14–35

Netherlands: appreciation of currency, 71, 85; commodity concentration of exports, 34; commodity-weighted share of world trade, 42; growth rate, 43; high export ratio, 47; population, 32; share in world exports, 55; size of domestic product, 33; trade ratio, 30, 34

New Zealand: agglomeration tendencies, relation to free trade area, 112; borrowing overseas capital, 43; commodity concentration of exports, 34; customs drawback union, 116–117; dependence on United Kingdom market, 34, 35, 40; high geographic concentration of exports, 47; import licensing, 65n; staple exports, percentages, 41

New Zealand-Australia Free Trade Agreement, 115–116

Nicholson, J. S., 86, 87, 89

Nigeria, size of domestic product, 33

Nordic Council, 114

Nordic customs union, 113–114

Norway: borrowing overseas capital, 43; commodity concentration of exports, 34; commodity-weighted share of world trade, 42, 78; EEC, EFTA, and, 112–113; proximity to major markets, 5; trade ratio, 30, 34

Nyasaland, 120

Ohlin, Bertil, 17

Oligopolistic competition, effects of customs union on, 99, 102, 106, 119

Orcutt, Guy, 69n, 80–81, 84, 123

Ostlind, Anders, 15

Pakistan, size of domestic product, 33

Pearce, Ivor F., 84

Perroux, François, 111

Polarization of industries, 111–112, 116–117, 120–121, 127

Population, 128–130t, 131–133t; as criterion of size, 4, 4n, 9, 12–13, 32–33, 41, 103, 104

Prebisch, Raul, 119n, 120

Product differentiation, 125

Productive capacity, 3; as criterion of nation size, 6–7, 87, 89–90, 123; in Graham model, 11, 87, 89–90, 123

Protectionist trade policies, 18–19

Purchasing power parity exchange rates, 24, 31

Ratio of international trade to national product, 22–35

Regional trade groups, see Customs union, European Economic Community, European Free Trade Area, Free trade areas

Reynolds, Mark W., 53n, 65n

Rhodesia, 120

Riemer, S., 43n

Robinson, E. A. G., 3, 11n, 103, 109

Rome Treaty, objectives, 112

Rothschild, K. W., 5, 99–100, 107n

Salant, William, 10, 55–56, 60, 61–62

Scandinavian countries, EEC and EFTA effects on, 113–114, 117

Scitovsky, Tibor, 18, 19, 100–101, 102, 105, 106, 107–108, 110

Sino-Soviet bloc, 24

Size, see Nation size

Size pessimism, 126

Index

Smith, Adam, 3, 6n
South Africa, 31, 32, 121; overseas lending as proportion of gross national product, 43; United Kingdom trade, 35
Soviet countries, excluded in studies, 31
Specialization, 6–7, 14, 17, 18n, 20, 21–22, 99, 100, 110, 112, 113, 120; in a Graham model, 91, 92
Springboard thesis 18
Stability of national income 16, 36–52, 125
Staley, Charles E., 118
Sterling area, 85
Streeten, P. P., 75n
Svennilson, I., 50
Swan, T. W., 40
Sweden: commodity-weighted share of world exports, 42; depression, effect on, 46; EEC, EFTA, and, 113–114; exports of finished durable goods, 20; largest supplier in world of its main export products, 78; newsprint and pulp exports, 41; proximity to major markets, 5; size of domestic product, 33
Switzerland: competition with Scandinavian firms, 114; export orientation of industry in, 18; exports, finished durable goods, 20; growth rate, 43; proximity to major markets, 5; stability, 50, 125; watch, precision instrument, and machinery industries, 103

Tariff bargaining, 15
Tariff barriers, 100, 101–102, 103, 117, 118, 119
Tariff-free areas, 105
Tariff reduction, 113, 114, 115
Tariffs: customs drawback union and, 117; economies of scale, 19; non-discriminatory tariffs in Europe, 15
Tarshis, L., 9–10
Tinbergen, Jan, 69n, 98, 123
Trade, absence of empirical studies on critical aspects of, 96
Trade barriers, effect on trade, 95, 126
Trade dependence, 34, 35, 36–52; on imports, 36–37; on imports of fixed capital goods, 37–38; on fluctuation of real income, 40, 44–46; on other countries for economic growth, 42–43; on overseas prices, 40–42
Trade Expansion Act of 1962, 115
Trade gap, 40, 65, 126
Trade ratios: and trade dependence, 36, 45; in a Graham model, 95; of small nations, 14–35
Trade statistics, small developed countries, 33t
Triffin, Robert, 18, 105
Tsiang, S. C., 57n, 72, 84

United Kingdom: Australian trade and, 35; competition for Scandinavian firms, 114; Danish trade and, 35; EEC and, 34; exports, finished durable goods, 20, 24; growth rate, 43; imperial preference, 34; New Zealand trade and, 34, 35; small country trade and, 34, 47; South African trade and, 35
United Nations: per capita incomes, 31; *Yearbook of National Accounts Statistics*, 23, 24
United States: Canada-U.S. Free Trade Arrangement, 114–115, 117; depression, effect on, 46; exports, finished durable goods, 20; gross domestic product, 32–33; growth rate, 43; import ratio, 54; small country trade and, 34; Venezuelan trade and, 35

Venezuela: dependence on U.S. market, 35; devaluation of currency, 71; exports,

index of concentration, 34; high geographic concentration of exports, 47; overseas lending as proportion of gross national product, 43
Verdoorn, P. J., 105
Vietnam, trade ratio, 30
Viner, Jacob, 97, 102–103

Wallich, H. C., 53n, 65n
Weiler, J., 10, 42
West Germany: exports, finished durable goods, 20; import ratio, 54; small country trade and, 47; *see also* Germany
Whitin, T. M., 90n

Yntema, Theodore, 79n
Young, Allyn, 110

N